PRAISE FOR THE LAST TIPI

"*The Last Tipi* gives the reader a powerful key to unlocking the story each of us—young or old, living or dying—holds tightly to our heart. As Kris Landry explains so movingly, keeping it locked up does no one any good."—Jim Trelease, NY Times best-selling author, *The Read-Aloud Handbook*, www.Trelease-on-Reading.com

"Kris Landry tells her life story with a liberating honesty. *The Last Tipi* is a magnificent testimony to acceptance, compassion, and love. I left this book with a greater respect for the generosity and power of the human spirit. It was a privilege to read this book."—Philip Glynn, MD, Director of Oncology, Mercy Medical Center, Springfield, MA; Medical Director, Noble VNA and Hospice, Westfield, MA; Asst. Clinical Professor of Medicine, Tufts Medical Center, Boston, MA

"What is addressed within the covers of *The Last Tipi* is beyond Kris's personal story. There is transference to humanity's longing for more compassion and love, embracing the vulnerable points of decision that effect a lifetime."—Ilizabeth Fortune, MA, CST, Founder and CEO , Institute of Creative Intelligence, www.IlizabethFortune.com

"*The Last Tipi* is a profound journey of faith, courage, and integrity that will open your heart. "—Rita Kinkelaar, APRN, Psychiatric Nurse Practioner

"*The Last Tipi* is Kris Landry's story about Story— hers and ours. Her lyrical writing pulls you into her soul's journey and invites you to take your own. Get ready for an amazing ride!"— Jennifer Rosenwald, #1 International Best Selling Co-Author, The Expert Success Solution, Speaker, Trainer, Business &

Personal Coach, www.JenniferRosenwald.com

"Kris beautifully integrates the power of telling your story with the transformative healing potential of simply releasing our deepest secrets. *The Last Tipi* leads you on a path of self-discovery and personal freedom! It's a must-read for reversing the impossible into the possible!" —Katie McLaughlin, Founder, Alchemy Wellness Center, Health and Wellness Consultant, Ashstanga Yoga Instructor, www.AlchemyWellness.com

"When I read *The Last Tipi*, I burst into tears—for Kris Landry and her courage, and tears for myself, because I knew I needed to go into *The Last Tipi* and release the chains that bound me. This book is for anyone who wants to become whole."—Michele Accettulli, Coordinating Manager, New York City Health & Hospitals

"I offer many blessings for Kris's book, *The Last Tipi*. It will help many people."—Geshe Chongtul Rinpoche, Lama of the Tibetan Bon Tradition, Spiritual Director of Bon Shen Ling, www.BonShenLing.org

"Kris Landry's *The Last Tipi* will transform the way you view your life. From my own experience, many times I thought I had entered *the last tipi* to tell the story of how my life had played out. Marriage, children, corporate success, divorce, remarriage, loss. None of those ended my story. They were just chapters. Landry's book poignantly reminds us that as long as we have breath, we can endlessly enter into that tipi and create a different ending for our own book of life. "—Scott Carbonara, "The Leadership Therapist," Speaker, Author, Consultant, CEO, Spiritus Communications, www.LeadershipTherapist.com

Also By M. Kris Landry

THE EXPERT SUCCESS SOLUTION

Co-Author

For Pamela, Sandra and
Quigley! You are wonderful hosts,
and we enjoyed our stay very much.
You listen to Amanda's stories
all through the year. Please share
here is one more. Please share
with anyone you think this
book will serve. Blessings 6/11
Kris

THE LAST TIPI

A Journey to Healing
Through Storytelling

M. Kris Landry
Former Hospice Chaplain

THE LAST TIPI: A JOURNEY TO HEALING THROUGH STORYTELLING

ISBN-13: 978-0692796603

Cover Design by: George Foster

Interior Design by: Amanda Rae Heinrich

Published by: Spiritus Communications

"There is no greater agony than bearing an untold story inside you."

—*Maya Angelou*

DEDICATION

FOR LARRY, THE HOLDER OF THE STORYTELLER'S HEART

TABLE OF CONTENT

INTRODUCTION

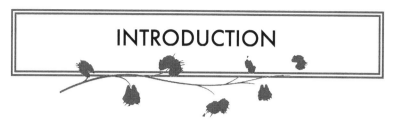

Native Americans, indigenous peoples, have traditionally encouraged their people to visit in tipis and share stories about their lives. They could do this many, many times and would always be welcomed by their neighbors. But a day would come when the storyteller would get sick of telling the old story again and again and would know that it was time to enter into "The Last Tipi," a place to tell the old story that had defined that person and left him or her feeling stuck in life one last time, and leave it there. And when the storytellers left "The Last Tipi," they would take with them the wisdom they had gained from the past, walk into the present, and dream a new story.

I loved this tradition immediately when a healer friend shared it with me. It reminded me of my own story. I hadn't realized how important it was to know my story in the first place. I thought that life happened, and there was nothing I could do about it. I thought I should just pick myself up and move on from each life event.

For many years of my life, that's exactly what I did. I thought I had it all, whatever "having it all" meant, until one day when I realized that those parts of my story that I hadn't looked at were actually running my life in ways I had never imagined. I had a loving husband, two wonderful children, a beautiful home, a cat, a dog, two horses, and a life to be envied. But I couldn't feel "me." I went to college in my thirties, became a chaplain in my forties, and worked with a healer who told me I had attracted everything in my life and that until I understood this, I had no power to change. I worked with another healer in England who told me that it's all about lineage, and that if I didn't know the story of my family, everything I had ever run from would repeat itself.

And so I began to open my heart in a quest to connect to the part of myself I hadn't uncovered, and my stories poured out. For a while, this process seemed incredibly overwhelming; but as I told the stories again and again, I began to feel release. Soon I felt stronger. Eventually, there came a time when I could let the story go and write a new one.

Writing this story took many years. Each time I finished a chapter or two, I'd share it with my family and friends who would encourage me to write more. I did this again and again. At one point, I actually thought I had finished this work, only to realize how much I had left out. So back to the writing I went.

However, there came a day when I knew I had finally written my whole story. I had let it all out and could begin living my life in a freer way. The old story running in my head had been silenced at last, and I could begin to write a new story…a story about reclaiming my power. When I heard the tradition of "The Last Tipi," my heart leapt. YES, I thought, that's what I have done. I have gone to the soul of my story and dared to tell myself the truth. And once I finally lived in my truth, I could begin to feel free and live a new way.

So, I invite you, too, into "The Last Tipi." Maybe, as you read along, your story will surface, and you will lovingly take the time to honor your journey and release what no longer needs to be held.

PROLOGUE

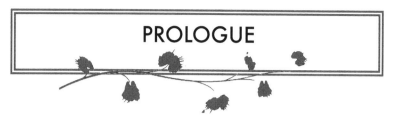

A beautiful May day in South Hadley, Massachusetts, provided the perfect setting for my graduation from Mount Holyoke College as a Frances Perkins Scholar. It seemed like only yesterday that I had entered Mount Holyoke's program for non-traditional students at the age of thirty-nine. I was incredibly proud I had earned my degree while married and raising two teenagers. Our commencement speaker was the revered Maya Angelou, author of *I Know Why The Caged Bird Sings*. I had read that book and some of her poetry, but on this day I experienced first-hand this incredible African-American woman reciting poems, singing songs, and sharing stories about her life.

I was captivated by the depth of her voice, but she ended her speech with a question that left a deep impact on me. Talking about women making a difference in the world, she said, "It doesn't matter what it looks like, or what color or shape it has. It just matters that you try to make a difference."

"Will it be you?"

CHAPTER 1
WHAT DOES A CHAPLAIN DO?

After graduation from Mount Holyoke College, I returned to taking care of my family full time. I had worked so hard and for so long in school, and then it was over. I felt a bit lost for a while.

Unlike a twenty-something woman graduating from college with a clean slate before her, I was returning to an already-created life and family. For many months, I just enjoyed not having to meet the agenda of professors and advisors.

However, in college, I had become accustomed to the intensity of personal challenge and growth—and found that I needed it. I yearned to be doing something useful and fulfilling. So I sought and found that intensity again. I applied to a program called Clinical Pastoral Education or CPE. In a nutshell, the program prepares the participant for chaplaincy. After submitting an autobiography and filling out an extensive application, I was thrilled to be accepted.

The CPE Center I attended was led by Catholic clergy. However, CPE is a non-denominational training program. Students were happy to fulfill one unit of CPE credit, which could take up to five months to complete, feeling they had received incredibly useful tools for understanding themselves as well as others. Some attendees were clergy members finishing their work at divinity school and needing to take a unit in order to graduate. Others like me, however, became consumed with desire to become certified chaplains.

One day into the program, I felt my nerves come alive as I was struck with the reality of what I said I wanted to do. What on earth had I been thinking?

There were eight of us in the daytime class. We would meet one full day per week and share the experiences we had during our eight-hour, clinical-pastoral obligation at a given facility. In the beginning, there were training films and exercises to be taken home that challenged us to look at the inner workings of our lives. These would be shared with the class the next week.

The rationale for requiring that we share our own life stories was that understanding our journeys was essential to accompanying others. We needed to ensure that our own issues and feelings would not get in the way of offering the type of pastoral care that would allow others to find meaning and a sense of Spirit's presence and activity in their own lives.

In our interaction with patients, we were required to write what was called a verbatim report about our patient conversations while conducting each visit. We would describe everything we observed about the patient, including the environment, relating what we heard and saw as best we could. In this process, I gained new insight into the meaning of sharing—as I not only reported on the patient during the visit, but also the experience I was having as the chaplain.

The director of the program, David Bolton, SJ, was an extraordinary man who introduced me to Carl Jung's teachings. He opened my eyes to the awareness that there was a consciousness within me. Kathleen Foley, SND, was his assistant—and the glue that kept everything together and organized. A gifted and dedicated woman, she taught me to cherish my growing edges.

I'll never forget the day she said, "Kris, I think you'd be good on the hospice floor."

"Why?" I quickly asked her.

"Well," she said, "you wrote about your mother dying in the autobiography portion of your application to the CPE program, so it seems that would be a good placement for you."

There was nothing I could do except start to sweat! But I agreed to give it a try.

I was assigned to a small hospital in Westfield, Massachusetts. As I pushed open the double doors to the hospice unit, my chest grew heavy. It was hard to breathe. If I live through this, I thought, I can live through anything!

Sister Dorothy Walsh, my supervisor, was a woman who didn't waste words. White-haired and a bit bent-over, she brought compassion to everyone she met. When she walked down the hospital corridors, patients and staff would greet her with reverence. She would bend to touch a patient's arm, and immediately, tears would slide down her face. Patients gazed back at her with love in their eyes. Later, she would tell me she had the "gift of tears."

During my first day on her floor, Sister Dorothy welcomed me and sent me on my way to visit my first patient, a woman of my age whose diagnosis left her only a few months to live. One eye had been lost to cancer. She weighed about four hundred pounds. There was an enormous hoist in the room that lifted her into and out of bed.

I walked into the room, and out of my mouth came, "Isn't it a beautiful day?!"

"How would I know?" she responded. "I can't turn around to look out the window!"

I wrote up that visit for my verbatim report. I made copies for my supervisor and for each member of the group so they could read the patient's lines. I also read the chaplain's lines I had recorded after my visit with the patient. At the end of my report, the group offered constructive criticism regarding my compassionate responses and whether I was truly listening to what the patient was saying.

I became acutely aware of how high my voice could be pitched when I was nervous, and of how I needed to wear one of my many masks to shield my insecurity. I realized that I didn't know how to listen to another person for any length of time; that if it was too painful to hear what someone was saying, I might laugh nervously. I was so disconnected from my own feelings of abandonment and helplessness that it was impossible for me to be with a person who was anticipating her death.

This marked the beginning of scratching the surface of my well-maintained public persona of perfection. I thought I was going to learn how to be a chaplain to others when, in fact, I was going to learn how be a chaplain to myself.

For me, at that time, there seemed to be no redemption in writing papers of self-reflection. I would write about my family of origin and think, So what am I supposed to do with this? But Kathleen's reference to my mother's death had knocked at the locked door of my pain and suffering. I had lived life into my early forties from a place in which my code of conduct was predicated on the notion that there was nothing I could do about anything that had happened in my childhood. That was that! Issues closed! I just went on.

But once the chipping away began, my feelings—feelings that I had never before allowed myself to feel or express—came to the surface. I was like a moth to the flame. I wanted to go into the fire, and at the same time, I knew my life as I had known it was never going to be the same. Whatever had been holding back my repressed feelings was going up in ashes.

CHAPTER 2
MY NAME IS MAUREEN

My name is Maureen. I am the second child born to teenaged parents; my brother, Howard, thirteen months older than I, is severely developmentally challenged. My father abandoned my family when I was a baby. He was never heard from again. My mother became very ill and suffered a physical and mental breakdown. Unable to care for my brother, she gave total custody of him to the Commonwealth of Massachusetts. I was cared for by relatives, but I also spent time in foster care and an orphanage. I was about two years old when I was returned to my mother.

My CPE assignment was to write my family-of-origin story in one paragraph. I could have been writing that scenario to anyone. It was just a story. I was so detached from my emotions that my account didn't seem real. But it was my story, and I was being asked to look at it, go into it, and talk about it.

The thing was, I had always been filled with utter sadness and helplessness when it came to my mother. Orphaned at ten years old and relocated to foster care, my mother's self-esteem suffered into adulthood. Although beautiful, she was insecure and emotionally fragile.

When I was a little girl, I absolutely adored my mother and crumbled inside when she cried—which she did often for many reasons. My father's abandonment of us had left my mother in complete despair. We were on welfare. And, I was never allowed to tell anyone that I had a brother; any mention of him was forbidden. I learned at an early age how to shape others' perception of me.

When I was five years old, I was able to attend first grade, which allowed my mother to get a full time job. Her ability to work got us off of the welfare rolls and onto the top of a list for a subsidized apartment in a housing project. When our name was pulled, we celebrated. Life was getting better.

I was just a baby when my 22-year-old mother contracted a very serious case of diabetes. She needed to take insulin shots every day, and most days battled mood swings and emotional outbursts. I learned to run to her with a candy bar or a glass of orange juice when she was having an insulin reaction and needed some fast sugar to prevent convulsions.

One day, when I was a very little girl, my mother and I were on an errand, and she collapsed in the street. I remember looking at her on the ground, horrified, not knowing what to do. A car stopped, and two men— strangers to me—jumped out, put us in their backseat, and rushed us to a hospital. I waited in the corner of what seemed like a very large and noisy room, thinking, "She's not coming back this time." When she entered the room hours later, her searching face looked for me and dissolved me into tears. I was so happy and relieved that she was alive. We held each other for a long, long time.

When I was about to enter the third grade, my mother announced I'd be going away to a private school, and that I was very fortunate to have this opportunity. Indeed, I was. It was a small French academy in Salem, Massachusetts, run by nuns from France. She was able to provide this thanks to a friend who knew a priest who put in a good word to get me a scholarship. Many years later, I visited the school, which had become a campus for Salem State College, and was amazed at how small the property was. But when I was seven years old, I thought the campus was enormous. It had the most grass and trees I had ever seen!

I was a very, very quiet child, speaking only when spoken to. I had learned that it was safer to say nothing than to provoke an emotional outburst from my mother. She hated being asked questions like when, where, how, or why? When she announced that I'd be going away to school, I was speechless. I could not find my voice to ask any questions. I was already missing her. My mother and I simply took a long train ride to the strange new school, and she left me there.

I lived in a dormitory with children who ranged from first grade through high school. That's when the bedwetting started. I was mortified, but I was grateful for the kindness and care given to me by those nuns. Not a harsh word was ever spoken. Every night, I wet the bed. Every morning, my bed was changed. Never was I made to feel more humiliated than I already felt, and their unselfish kindness was new to me. Although my mother truly tried to be a good mother, she was often overwhelmed and needed to say just how hard it was to earn money to feed and clothe me. These sweet nuns never told me it was hard to change my sheets every day.

I lived for my mother to come back and get me on Friday afternoons. Five whole days away from her seemed endless. Friday could not come soon enough. I would look forward to the bag of potato chips she would give me for the ride home on the train.

One day, I was called to the office of Mother Superior and told that my mother was too sick to pick me up. I would have to stay at the school for the weekend. Not seeing my mother for two whole weeks seemed unbearable. There were no children at the school on the weekends, so after I attended Mass with the nuns in the morning, I was left to amuse myself. That Sunday evening, I was called to dinner and served fried eggs. I guess the look on my face told the sisters how surprised I was. They began to laugh. I told them I'd never had breakfast at night before. They very sweetly scavenged up some cold-cuts for a sandwich for me. It was my first experience with nuns who lived in a community and together would always help each other. To see them all fussing around me eased my longing to be home.

Many years later, I would experience this same giving quality when sisters from the convent my sister-in-law had once belonged to visited me just after my husband and I had our first child. They showed up unexpectedly; my house was a mess, because the baby was colicky and had kept me from sleeping for weeks. Five of them appeared at my door with great big smiles. When I invited them inside, they automatically began to fold the laundry and pack the dishwasher, and even volunteered to walk the baby. Their unselfishness so touched me that I experienced, maybe for the first time, an expansion of my heart—a feeling like love had grown within me somehow—that forever changed me.

I did pretty well in school, but I didn't always feel engaged. I remember being given a test sheet with questions and having no idea what the answers were or even what the subject was about. Like in the rest of my life, I often felt disconnected in school and spent a lot of time daydreaming. So it was a surprise to me when my grades were Bs or better.

The feeling of "not really being there" prevailed wherever I was…almost like I was in a daydream…and then I would realize: *Oh, I am here, and I need to take this test, or, My mother is unhappy with me, and I don't know what I did to cause it.*

As the months went by, I felt more comfortable, and the school started to feel like home. I would, however, be in for another surprise. At the end of the school year, my mother told me I wouldn't be returning to the academy. We would be moving to a new apartment on Commonwealth Avenue in Boston, Massachusetts. I felt very sad to be leaving the school. I had begun to make connections with other children. "Big sisters" from higher grades were assigned to us younger ones, and my big sister was a senior in high school. I don't remember her name, but I do remember one occasion when she wrapped her arms around me to comfort me – it was the day I learned that I wasn't going to return to the school. I absolutely loved her and was devastated that I would never see her again.

CHAPTER 3
A VOICE TO SING

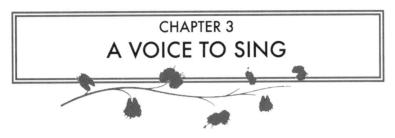

I remember the trolley going down the center of the street. I could watch it for hours from our top floor apartment. I would listen to screeching wheels on metal tracks and wonder where the passengers inside the trolley cars were going. The trolley, or the T, as it is called, still runs down Commonwealth Avenue in Boston today.

A new school, a new home, and a new boyfriend for my mother were in store for nine-year-old me. I handled the first two events pretty well, but the new boyfriend was another matter. My mother had dated before, and her gentlemen callers had always given me special attention. But this one was different.

His name was David. He was polite when he greeted me, but after that, he had nothing to say to me. He would invite us to dinner, and when we'd arrive at the restaurant, he'd get a table for me across the room from theirs. I thought it was strange, but going to dinner in a restaurant was such a rarity that I didn't say anything about it.

One night, feeling lonely at my own table, I ventured across the restaurant to theirs and asked my mother, "Does David like my red hair?" Everyone had always told me they loved my red hair.

Without skipping a beat, my mother responded, "No, Dear, he doesn't, because it's the color of his ex-wife's hair."

"Oh!" I said. I turned around and went back to my table. I knew I wouldn't be asking any more questions any time soon.

Several months later, my mother returned home with David after a weekend away and informed me that they had gotten married. "Oh," I said, and that was that.

I didn't know how to act with this person now living in my home every day. As I was going off to bed one evening during the first weeks of his being with us, I leaned over and kissed him goodnight, close to his lips.

My bed was a single box-spring and mattress pushed into an alcove in the kitchen. The space was wide open, and I could hear my mother and David talking in the living room. David was telling my mother he thought I was a very weird child for having kissed him goodnight that way.

Then he asked if she knew that I had told his niece that I had a severely developmentally challenged brother and that my mother was a diabetic. I knew that what I had overheard wouldn't bode well for my relationship with my mother or my new stepfather. My mother was furious that I had been so disloyal by telling our secrets. I heard her weeping and affirming David's opinion of me that I was a weird child. Lying in bed in that alcove in the kitchen, I just wanted to go to sleep so I wouldn't feel anything anymore. There was no one to turn to.

I had hoped I finally had someone to call Daddy, but his words that night to my mother hurt me deeply. I had always felt awkward around him, and he had never done anything to relieve those feelings. From that night on, I was never able to be myself around him again.

The next thing I knew, we were moving again—this time to New Hampshire. Even though David commuted to Boston for work, we needed to live outside of Massachusetts for two years after his divorce. In those days (at least that's what I was told), you had to wait two years before you could remarry. I assume it was legal in New Hampshire to marry sooner. (How times have changed!)

We rented a one-bedroom apartment on the top floor of an antique house. Across the hall, an elderly lady lived in the same amount of space as the three of us. David and my mother had the bedroom to themselves, and I had the box-spring and mattress, which doubled as the couch, in the living room. When it came time for me to sleep, I was ordered to roll over. David was quite specific about how my arms were to be folded, and I was never to turn in the direction of the television. He would bark his demands, and my mother would be silent. I would think: *She's got to know this is horrible for me.* But she never said a word.

My bedwetting returned. This was incredibly humiliating, especially now with a man in the house. My mother's response, although initially helpful, turned to anger about the extra laundry. She would wake me up several times during the night to go to the bathroom, but I still had a wet bed in the morning. Some nights, they'd put me to sleep in their bed, and I would wet that, too. I wanted to die, or at least disappear.

One day, we were in a department store, because my mother was looking for some new clothes. The saleswoman asked me, "What do you want, a sister or a brother?"

I told her I didn't know what she was talking about.

"Well, just look at your mother. Surely you know she's pregnant!"

26

And there she was, standing with a great, big belly. I felt so embarrassed that I hadn't known she was going to have a baby. When I asked her why she hadn't told me, she replied, "Oh, Maureen, why can't you figure these things out for yourself?"

My sister, Beverly, was born when I was ten years old. Four of us lived in a tiny, postage-stamp-sized apartment. With the new baby, my mother was emotionally drained—less and less able to make decisions for herself. Before marrying David, she had held down a full-time job, managed her diabetes, and cared for me on her own. But now, he dictated how things were to be done. It was as though she had given herself over to him, and I was expected to defer to him as well.

Marrying David offered my mother the security she had longed for. We owned a car, we could afford to buy steak to eat, and we could go out for ice cream on occasion. He paid all the bills! I can only imagine the relief my mother felt. But the other part of the bargain was that David never felt it necessary to give any reasons regarding his decisions. He just said *no* unless it suited him. He was not a bad man. He was a man of his generation in which he was the head of the household, and what he said was how things would be. I was clearly the baggage my mother had brought to the marriage, and she didn't want me to upset things.

We moved back to Massachusetts after two years and settled in a small town on the South Shore of Boston. For the first time in many years, I had a bedroom, which I shared with my baby sister. I went to public school from junior high through high school in that sleepy little town, which was the longest I had lived anywhere in my life.

It was there, at the age of eleven, that I discovered I could sing. I had thought everyone could sing. I was astonished when the choir director announced that I would be singing solo at Sunday Mass. My knees knocked from nerves. I was amazed that I actually did have a fine voice, and the more opportunities I had to use it in public, the better I felt about myself. This was from a girl who could not speak…it was as though all the feelings I couldn't express could now come through my soprano voice.

Throughout school, I took every invitation and opportunity to express myself that way. My singing became the foundation of my self-esteem. As a senior in high school, a college out West offered me a full music scholarship after its music director heard me sing.

My parents turned down that scholarship, announcing that instead I was going to go to work after high school. After all, my mother informed me, I owed David payment for all the food and clothes he had provided me over the years.

Nothing surprised me about my family anymore. At home, throughout my last year of high school, I felt depressed and wondered if I would actually survive living with my mother and stepfather. There seemed to be no visible exit sign.

My mother's health worsened after a miscarriage, which was followed by cancer of the cervix. She began drinking during the day and crying through the night. The sound of ice hitting the edge of a highball glass still makes me cringe. Throughout all of this, David seemed to be devoted to my mother. Only now, as I look back, I wonder, *Can I give him this credit?* At that time, I was completely absorbed in my own feelings of abandonment and couldn't understand what it was like for him to care for a sick wife and keep our household going. During those days, my actions revolved around not upsetting her. I was not allowed to ask questions of merit, discuss the local or national news, or offer any opinions about anything going on in the world. If I did happen to upset my mother, I was met with punishment, like withholding permission to attend a favorite school event or visit a friend after school.

During the middle of my senior year in high school, my parents announced that we'd be moving to a town nearer to Boston, closer to David's office. I lived with David's brother and his family in the same town and finished out the year, planning to join them after graduation.

The week before I graduated, the high school chorus gave their final concert. I had a solo. My mother and David did not attend. I remember singing from a deeply heartfelt place, because I loved the music and felt sad I'd soon be leaving school and friends. After the performance, two men from the audience approached me and complimented me on my singing. They said they were associates of Leonard Bernstein, and that Mr. Bernstein was visiting with his mother who lived in town. If I was interested, they would like to introduce me to Mr. Bernstein and have me sing for him. I told them I couldn't, because I was moving the following week and had a job waiting for me at an insurance company in Boston.

CHAPTER 4
THE HOME AWAY FROM HOME

At my first job, I met a wonderful friend, Alberta. I had taken a typing and stenography test at my high school that was submitted to several insurance companies in Boston, Massachusetts. I did very well on my test and was offered a job with the Prudential Insurance Company. Alberta had taken the same test at her high school and wound up in the same division with me.

We were the antitheses of each other: I was Irish and Swedish with fair skin, blue-eyes, and freckles. She was Lebanese and Syrian—and dark-skinned, with big, brown eyes and a gorgeous smile. Her family intrigued me with their large gatherings and the incredible smells from their never-ending cooking.

I learned so much from this new, dear friend. I had never been allowed to stay overnight at anyone's home before, but now I enjoyed, for the first time, the intimacy of a true friendship. She just accepted me as I was and thought I was beautiful. She even accepted me when I told her I was pregnant.

Unlike my mother—who screamed, cried, and ranted for days—Alberta simply asked, "How can I help you?"

I had been sexually active for about a year before I became pregnant. I couldn't believe it. I thought I'd been careful. I was fully developed by the time I turned twelve years old, and I'd become accustomed to a lot of attention from boys and men. Unaware that I was starved for attention and affection at home, the looks and whistles I received as a teenager proved all too alluring to me. The boys who asked me out were older and very experienced. With so much attention paid to my looks and body, I felt a power I had not known before. I wasn't invisible. In fact, I was desired. It wasn't long before this desire to be accepted and noticed got me into "trouble."

I'd had no education about sex or intimacy. The only advice my mother had ever given me about sex came one night as I was going out the door on a date. "You better not be having sex with your boyfriend," she warned me, "because all you do is spread your legs and you won't like it!" I was stunned. I knew I didn't want to talk about sex with her.

There was no chance of marrying the father of my baby. Through a friend of a friend, who knew a lawyer who handled such things, I was taken to a private adoption agency in southern Connecticut. There, I was asked what I wanted for my baby. The possibility of keeping my baby was never, ever mentioned. I couldn't imagine how I could raise a child on my own, so I considered the only option available: adoption. I was told that there was a very wealthy family that had one child and wanted another. They could give my baby everything under the sun. Since I believed that I could give my baby nothing, I agreed that this family would be a fine choice.

During this meeting, another decision was made: about my residential placement. At three months pregnant, I was ushered off to a home for unwed mothers in New York City. David drove me to New York, never saying a word along the way. I had no idea where I was going or who I'd be with. I still wasn't showing, so it was a shock even to me to be greeted by ten or so obviously pregnant girls my age at an incredibly beautiful home just off Park Avenue.

How ironic to have landed in such a place. There were three floors with a spiral staircase and an elevator in between. The first floor held an office, a visiting room, and two bedroom suites for staff. A dumb-waiter went from the large dining room and small kitchen area to the basement to pick up food prepared by the cook. On the second and third floors were dormitory-style bedrooms housing two to four women per room. On my first day, I was taken to the top floor and assigned to a two-person room. My roommate, Millie, showed me around. Then I curled up in a fetal position on my bed and slept for hours. Millie finally came and announced that dinner was being served; I needed to get up.

How comfortable these young women seemed to be as they talked about being pregnant, and about their boyfriends and families. I was amazed to hear that their families would be visiting them on the weekends.

I realized this was not the case for me. I was at that home for six months and never got a visit or telephone call. I once asked my family for and received about fifty dollars, but that was it for communication. I began to acknowledge that my family was truly detached from me.

These women allowed me to express my feelings and helped me to realize, at least by their example, that my life was going to go on. But before my life could go on, I had six months to think about the baby inside my belly and wonder how I would feel when giving it up. Everyone at the home had already agreed to give up their babies for adoption. Many, like me, also already had families waiting for their births. There was a strange comfort in our uncomfortable situation; it was one we shared, day and night.

However, about a month after I arrived, one girl suddenly announced that she had changed her mind about giving up her baby for adoption. This news sent waves of shock throughout the house. She had only been with us for a few days. Apparently, the conversations we all shared about adoption had rattled her. There was a big intervention by the staff. The girls in the home couldn't imagine changing their minds. I couldn't either, and I remember feeling scared to think about having a baby and being left alone without any help or support. That girl left the home within a day of her decision, and I don't know what happened to her. But it was then that I realized that you could only be at that home if you were relinquishing your rights as a mother.

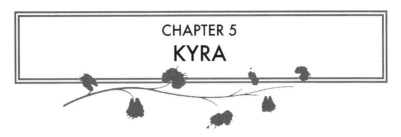

CHAPTER 5
KYRA

I was happy at the home. Strange as it sounds, it was my emancipation of sorts. It was my first time away from my mother and David. I actually began to blossom. I laughed and talked, voiced opinions, and became a bit of a leader. I got to know New York City and went to museums, delis, movies, and I walked and walked and walked. I felt like I was beginning to live a normal life, even through such an abnormal set of circumstances.

During the last three months at the home, I had three other roommates. Our babies were due within weeks and days of each other. One by one, we started to deliver. Millie delivered a boy. Next came Barbie with a girl. I was due on Christmas Day, but instead that's when Carole delivered her baby girl. I delivered a girl on December 27.

I awoke that morning to a huge contraction that left me no doubt about what was happening. I walked to the bathroom holding my big belly in my hands. Another contraction hit. I dressed quickly and went downstairs for the matron who would take me to the hospital. I found her standing at the bottom of the stairwell waiting for me. She said she'd heard the sound of my feet on the floor above her room and knew I must be ready to deliver.

It was 5:30 in the morning. The sun was just coming up. We walked down Fifth Avenue, and the doormen nodded as we passed by. I thought it was strange to be walking several blocks to the hospital to give birth and, at the same time, to be seeing these men tipping their hats and saying, "Good morning!" as if it were a normal day. The old German lady took me to Lenox Hill Hospital and deposited me at the registration desk. With that, she wished me luck and left. I could not have felt more alone or scared.

Upon admission, a ride in a wheelchair brought me to a single room where I disrobed and lay down on a table. After the nurse checked to see how many centimeters I was dilated, she left me alone in the room—closing the door behind her. I lay on the table looking up at the ceiling, wondering if anyone on the outside would remember I was in there about to deliver a baby. I had been given a shot in my bottom which made me feel sleepy.

Suddenly, the most incredible pain I had ever known hit me. I screamed. Sound kept billowing out of me. My knees lunged up into my chest. I thought, "There is a God! And I have no control over what my body is doing."

A nurse came bursting through the door, took one look at me, and barked loudly, "Why the hell were you left alone like this? Your water broke a while ago, and you were left to lie in it! I can't believe this," she muttered as she called staff to come and bring me to the delivery room. "Don't push!" she yelled, and soon a mask was put over my face. All I could hear was ringing in my ears and bells going off in my head. Then everything went black.

I woke up some time that afternoon in the maternity ward. *I guess I had a baby*, I thought to myself. There was a blaring television in the middle of the room. A soap opera character was yelling, "Don't take my baby; don't take my baby!!" I looked to my left, and there was Carole, cooing to her baby. And over to my right was Barbie, holding hers. A nurse noticed that I was awake and came to check on me. She informed me that I had a slight fever and therefore wouldn't be able to see or hold my baby. I asked her, "What did I have?" She told me she'd have to check.

The next morning, the nurses brought the new babies into the maternity ward for the mothers to feed. They lined up the bassinettes, and each mother retrieved her bundle. I got out of bed and found that there was one baby left to be claimed. "Well, you must be mine," I said. I checked her wristband, and my name was there.

For several days, Barbie, Carole, and I were roommates again. Millie would come to visit us. In those days, hospitals kept mothers for a week after delivery. I had seven days to hold, feed, and change my beautiful daughter, whom I named Kyra.

For the last two days in the hospital, I was alone without my friends. I hadn't heard from my parents, although I was told they'd be informed. I wondered how I would get through what I knew I still had to do.

On the day the social worker was coming for her, I dressed Kyra and got her ready. Then, I went downstairs to the administrative floor to sign the papers that would allow my baby's adoption to take place. The woman behind the desk was kind and sensitive to what I was doing. I was surprised by the attention she was giving me. When she looked at me and said, "Are you sure this is the only thing you can do?" I signed my name as fast as I could and pretty much ran onto the elevator.

I was on the third floor, and the elevator was going down. I needed to go up, but I stayed on anyway. I was standing there, deep in my own thoughts, when I heard the piercing cries of a baby at the back of the elevator. I turned around and saw Kyra in the arms of the social worker. The elevator stopped at the first floor. They got off, with the cries of Kyra floating through the closing doors. I thought I would faint. I went to my room and passed out on my bed.

The next day, I was discharged from the hospital and scheduled to spend several more days at the home before my family picked me up. Everyone I had known was already gone. New young women were arriving, looking like I had six months before.

CHAPTER 6
THIS IS THE MOMENT

David arrived to pick me up. The car was waiting outside. I got into the car to find my mother and sister sitting there. My mother smiled at me, and my sister said, "Hi, do you know that we're going to the New York World's Fair today?"

I walked around the fair feeling like a crazy person.

As we drove back to Massachusetts, I fell silent. I had no idea what to say to anyone. They, on the other hand, knew what they wanted to say to me: "Get a job right away!" After all, I was told, I needed to pay room and board.

I had stepped right back into their awful world, and now it would be mine again. If I hadn't had Alberta to call and visit upon my return, I would have lost my mind.

One week later, I got a job at a real estate firm in Boston. Sitting at my desk, I thought, "My God, does anyone know that I've just had a baby?" I vowed to myself that I would never forget the baby daughter I had birthed. With all of my aching heart, I would love her forever.

There was almost no comment at home about my having a baby. I asked my mother why she hadn't written or called while I was away, and she said that it had been too depressing to think about.

While in New York, I had written for and received information about the Berklee College of Music in Boston. When I returned to Massachusetts, I enrolled as a part-time evening student taking singing and theory lessons.

My mother went crazy when she discovered this! "I told you not to be thinking about college; and if you don't do what we say, we've decided to turn you over to the state as a delinquent child!"

Could they possibly do that to me, I wondered, *when I'm eighteen years old?*

I took the classes at Berklee anyway. Music told me I was alive. I got gigs here and there. I passed as older than I was, so I was able to get jobs singing in nightclubs where I technically was supposed to be twenty-one to abide by liquor laws.

I began to work with an arranger whose studio housed others in the music business. After my session one day, I entered the waiting area to find a man who turned out to be a booking agent. He asked me what I did. He wanted to know what my singing range was and if I would be interested in auditioning for a folk group sponsored by the Prince Spaghetti Company.

"Yes, oh yes," I replied, "I would be very interested!" Our conversation caused me to miss my regular train. I got home an hour later than usual. I found that my mother had been taken to the hospital in an ambulance. Apparently, she had become hysterical because I hadn't come home at the designated time to set her hair.

I auditioned for the singing group and got the job. We were five men and two women. They had been singing together for several years and had been an opening act for Gerry Vale. I was in heaven! I quit my day job and changed my name. My booking agent told me, "Maureen Publicover just won't make it as a headliner." I said I was fine about changing my name and decided to call myself "Kris Kover." We performed in nightclubs, at colleges, and on radio and television.

I asked myself, "Could this really be my life, happy at last?"

I sang with the group for a year and a half. It was called "The Prince Spaghetti Minstrels." No kidding. We were the headliners appearing at the Outside In nightclub near Fenway Park in Boston. We did three sets a night, seven nights a week. We worked hard for our money, not at all like a college concert that brought easy money.

The first night we appeared there, I arrived in a blue mini-dress with white stripes down the sides, go-go boots, and long, tossed hair covering one eye. I had to pass the bar to get to the dressing room. A guy in a trench coat having a drink looked over at me and asked, "Hey, who won the game, little girl?"

I looked away and mumbled under my breath, "Asshole!"

The guy in the trench coat sent drinks to me after each set. At the end of the night, I had all the drinks lined up on a table. I didn't drink much anyway, but when I was working, I didn't drink at all. Eventually, the guy came over to me, looked at the drinks on the table, and asked, "What *do* you drink?"

"Tea!" I answered

"Well then, can I take you out for a cup of tea?" he asked.

"I'll miss my ride home," I told him.

"I'll drive you home," he offered. I asked him his name and went downstairs to the dressing room.

"Hey, does anybody know a guy named Larry Landry?" I asked.

All five men from my singing group turned around at the same time and said, "You mean Super Scooper? We don't know what that guy does, but the girls just love him."

I told them he'd offered to take me out for a cup of tea and then take me home. I wanted to know if they thought he was okay.

"Oh, sure," was the answer. So off we went at one o'clock in the morning to get a cup of tea.

Super Scooper, or Larry, was the funniest person I'd ever met. No wonder the girls sat around him giggling all night. He read me like a book, pointing out that he could see I was jealous that the other girl singer had more songs. And what was even funnier was that he laughed at himself as much as he laughed at everyone else. He had this innate sense about people that he could transform into comedy.

Two nights later, he showed up at the Outside In again. He didn't send drinks this time, but during one of my breaks, he said he had something to ask me. We went to a not-so-private place beside the bar, behind a keg of beer. "Now, you don't have to answer me right away; just think about this for a while," he said, and asked me to marry him.

Obviously, I thought he was nuts, and I just laughed at him. Before I could say anything, he said, "I know you love me; it's just a matter of time before you'll know it!" I had never met anyone with an ego that large. Then he said, "I had a dream that I would meet a girl singer and marry her!" I told him I thought he was crazy, but I was laughing when I said it.

Five months later, I married him.

The Minstrels worked as an opening act on several occasions. The performance I remember most vividly was opening for The Beach Boys at the University of Massachusetts. There were thousands of people in the auditorium. I felt incredible singing to such a huge audience.

Fifteen years later, I was asked to open for a Bob Hope performance at the Springfield Civic Center in Springfield, Massachusetts. The group that sponsored his appearance asked me two days before his arrival if I was up for it. "You bet!" I told them. At the last moment, I was informed that Mr. Hope always had "God Bless America" sung before his shows. I remember Larry driving me to the Civic Center in the pouring rain, teaching me the words.

The opportunity for me to open for a headliner appeared again in 1997 when Larry's real estate service was scheduled to host a convention in Las Vegas. Before the trip, Larry and I were having dinner with Alan, the president of the real estate service, when the subject of entertainment came up. The practice of the real estate service had been to have someone within the real estate service family perform before the main attraction. After a couple of glasses of wine, I remarked that I'd love to be the opening act. Alan said, "Kris, you've got the job, and you're going to be opening for Tom Jones!"

I chose to sing "This Is the Moment" from the Broadway musical "Jekyll and Hyde." It's a great, big, wonderful, song that modulates as the intensity of the music increases, so by the end of the song, I would be singing full-voiced in my strongest vocal range. It's a very dramatic delivery. I sent a copy of my music to Mr. Jones's music director with the notation that I needed to sing the song a half-step down from the written key.

I bought a fabulous blue gown with matching shoes and made appointments for my hair and makeup to be done once I arrived in Las Vegas. In the meantime, I practiced, practiced, and practiced my song until it became a part of me.

Once we landed in Las Vegas, I could feel the nerves taking hold. In hindsight, it was my one true experience of being a diva. It wasn't pretty. I was breaking out in hives. I had a sound-check rehearsal with Tom Jones's staff and began to realize how big a deal this show was going to be. This experience was going to be more than anything I'd ever known on stage.

I couldn't eat. I couldn't stay out of the bathroom. I couldn't be pleasant. My nerves were running wild inside of me. People were sending notes and flowers offering me wishes of good luck, but I was suffering in my self-imposed diva-hood! Finally, the evening arrived on the last night of the convention. After some pleasant talk from Alan, I was introduced to thunderous applause. I began my walk from the main floor of the convention center, under a spotlight, and ascended a staircase to the ballroom's stage! I walked slowly in my three-inch heels, thinking, *Maureen, this is the last time I will do this to you. I never need this much attention in my life again!*

The spotlight followed as I walked to the center of the stage, microphone in hand. The velvet curtain was closed. I was to listen for the piano introduction to my music from behind the curtain, which would cue me to begin. I looked out and couldn't see anyone, because the spotlight was in my eyes. I said hello and told the audience I was thrilled to be there to sing what I thought was a special song for them.

As I was speaking, I realized there wasn't any sound coming from behind the curtain. I couldn't believe what was happening, or more to the point, not happening. I started to talk to the audience and share with them how I'd rehearsed with the piano player earlier and that I was sure he would show up soon. But there was no piano player backstage! The audience wasn't quite sure what I meant. I could tell they were wondering if what I was saying was part of the act. I smiled and continued to speak, as I walked from one end of the stage to the other. The audience began to catch on. I could hear some laughter and then some clapping. Alan came back on stage. The place filled with cheering voices. He announced that I'd be back in a few minutes while they found where the piano player had disappeared to!

Standing behind the curtain, wondering how I was going to survive the evening, I looked over and saw the piano player running down the back aisle of the stage, looking apoplectic. He'd been having a beer at the bar waiting for someone to come and get him. I couldn't look at him. I heard myself being re-introduced. Out I went, again, onto the stage. This time, the piano player played the introduction to my music. But immediately, I knew something was wrong. He played the song in the original key, not the key a half-step lower which fit my voice. That meant I'd begin the song in the middle of my singing range instead of at its bottom. When the song modulated up, I would be headed towards my long-lost coloratura ability.

It was my moment. How surreal! I was singing—and thinking about the big, fat notes at the end that I didn't think I could reach. I did the best I could. The place erupted with applause and cheer. I was mercifully escorted off the stage. Back at my table, I listened to Tom Jones do his stuff. The piano player never made any mistakes. When the evening was over, I just wanted to go to our room, get out of the blue dress and shoes, and promise I'd never do this to myself again. But first, I was surrounded by friends congratulating me on a fine singing job. I was praised for being able to stand on my feet in a difficult situation and apparently not show the terror I'd felt. All of this happened thirty-plus years after my involvement with the Prince Spaghetti Minstrels.

Getting back to when I met Larry: I had already been thinking beyond the Minstrels. I knew the group would disband before long, and I was thinking of going to New York City to try to get work as a singer. That's when Larry became incredibly persuasive about getting married. I had to say yes. In the beginning, I loved him mainly because he made me laugh. I had never known spontaneous laughter in my life; I couldn't say no to the laughter. It was that simple.

But it would be years before I would realize how deeply I loved him. I told him about the events that had shaped me: including having Kyra. He thought I'd been courageous to tell him. After meeting and being with my parents, he also said he didn't know how I had survived living with them. In time, I realized he loved me because I was me—something I hadn't experienced much in my life previously.

CHAPTER 7
MY MOTHER

We had a tiny wedding, with Alberta as my maid-of-honor.

My mother had been sure no one would ever want me and taunted me with, "I bet you haven't told Larry about the baby, have you? He won't want you if he knows!"

The night Larry was coming to the house to tell my parents about our plans to marry, he was caught in a snowstorm a state away. My mother took his not coming as an insult. The following week when he finally came, she refused to come out of her room to speak with him.

David and my mother cashed in my life insurance policy and bought themselves clothes for the wedding. They offered us a broken television as a gift. David asked Larry for my last two weeks room and board the night before my wedding. When our wedding day came, I thought, "I never have to live with this insanity again."

Living in our own home, not experiencing daily toxic dumping—instead receiving love, humor, companionship, intimacy, and the visceral experience of my heart opening—brought a joy I had never known. I realized that things didn't have to be right or wrong, black or white, sad or depressing. With Larry, every day was met with a joy for life, whether in cooking, taking a ride in his convertible, or dreaming about our future together. Almost five decades later, Larry is still my best friend.

Our lives grew together. We bought our first home and then our second. I didn't know Larry was part Gypsy; he could move at the drop of a hat! All through his childhood, his mother would pack up their apartments or homes and have the family ready to move in two days. Larry's sister, Celine, tells the story of when she was in eighth grade and announced to her teacher she'd be moving before Christmas. The teacher arranged a going away party for her. She received many little gifts by which to remember her class. The family moved to another city an hour away. Before two months were up, their mother wanted to move back. Celine wound up in the same eighth grade class. She felt so embarrassed. She wondered if she should return the gifts.

We were married for four years when our daughter, Joan Marie, was born. Two years later, our son, Michael Daniel, arrived. We had moved again, this time to western Massachusetts near Springfield, the place of Larry's birth and early schooling. Within a year, Larry was selling real estate and soon opened his own company. He was a natural at selling homes and putting buyers and sellers at ease. It was his gift. Our life in the suburbs was tranquil. Years later, when our daughter attended college in Boston, she criticized us for having raised her in a community that lacked diversity. She was, in fact, right. We had. But for me, it was like living in a peaceful kingdom.

My stepfather died of a heart attack several years after our son was born. My mother's health also spiraled downward with renal failure, blindness, an amputated leg, and several mini-strokes. I tried to be helpful, but it was hard because I lived two hours away, and because visiting my mother in the hospital often left me feeling overwhelmed with sadness for her...and for myself. My sister, Beverly, was very affected by our parents' bizarre attitudes about people, and absorbed their notions about what she was supposed to fear and avoid in life. It had a paralyzing effect on her. Although she tried to be helpful, she was lost in a failing marriage and struggling to keep herself emotionally balanced. The only time we seemed to be together was when standing on opposite sides of our mother's hospital bed while visiting her.

My mother's last two years of life were spent in hospitals which she didn't want to leave. She nearly died a couple of times, but was resuscitated—something she later told me she was very angry about (this, from a woman who had been morbidly afraid of dying since I could remember). I learned to appreciate the Do Not Resuscitate forms hospitals began offering patients upon admittance; if this form had been available when my mother was hospitalized, her signature could have saved her from further suffering.

Several months before my mother died, she said to me, "I'm sorry your life was so hard, Maureen. I shouldn't have let David treat you the way he did."

I managed to answer, "It's all right, Mom; you did the best you could do." It was all I could say in the moment. She was so sick, weak, and tired. I couldn't be unkind to her. The truth was, I loved her, and always had. She had been orphaned at ten years old and had no model of how to love her children in a healthy way. She wanted and needed love for herself. She did not have an abundance to give, but instead a void she needed to have filled. If only she had known how much I had always loved her. When I would tell her, she would tell me I was a liar just like my father. As a child, and as an adult, this was terrible to hear. I had nowhere to go emotionally when I was told I was like the father I had never known. Frankly, these words just wrecked me. A small voice inside would say: *Am I really just like him?* I could never answer that question.

One day, I got a call from my mother's doctor telling me she was refusing to go to dialysis. She'd been going for eight years, and the process had become more and more painful. She told me in fact that it had become more painful to live than to die.

I spoke to her and asked her to please go for her treatment. I said I'd be there to see her in two days. She weakly said, "Okay." However, when she arrived at the dialysis unit, she again refused to participate.

When the doctor called again, I asked him if my mother had the right to say no to the process. He said that she could refuse to take dialysis, which would definitely lead to her death; but a next-of-kin had to give the final word. So there I was, in that awful moment, not knowing what was right or wrong, but knowing that my mother had certainly lived her share of pain.

I said to the doctor, "If my mother doesn't want to take the dialysis, then I will honor her decision." And that was that. My mother died five days later. It was over. When I buried her beside David, I thought, "I'm really on my own now."

I can still remember looking at the gravesite and thinking, "I'm never coming back here again." And I never have gone back. Something in me said: *This is finished, and I can go on now.* The battle was over—my mother's battle with her mental and physical health, and my battle of trying to be seen by her as a daughter who truly loved her.

I kept waiting for something to happen to me. Everyone kept talking about grieving and how it might take years to process my mother's death. But, I felt okay. I even felt a little guilty about being so okay. I rationalized I had grieved about my mother so much during my life that there was nothing left, not even tears. I think I had already distanced myself emotionally in order to survive.

It had not been long since my mother's death when I heard Sister Kathleen say, "Kris, you wrote about your mother dying in your autobiography; so it seems that hospice would be a good placement for you."

CHAPTER 8
HOSPICE STORIES

After two years at Western Massachusetts Hospital in Westfield, Massachusetts, I was assigned to Baystate Medical Center in Springfield, Massachusetts, to continue my clinical-pastoral work in hospice care. The unit was shaped in a large U, with the nurse's station and activity rooms at the bottom. The long-term care patients, who were either unable to go home or too sick to be in nursing homes, had rooms on one side. The hospice care patients lived on the other side. These patients became like family to the hardworking staff. Periodically, I would meet with the nurses who kept me informed about what was going on in the lives of their charges. There were patients who welcomed a visit from me, and some who preferred not to be disturbed. Some patients had families who visited regularly, and some patients had no visitors at all. There were patients who had reviewed and reflected upon their lives and were at peace with their situations and patients who were still in shock that their lives could be ending soon. I would visit each one.

I had no idea how listening to these end-of-life stories would impact me. My hope was to bring a healing presence to these patients, but what I discovered was that their love and trust often times healed me. Their vulnerability deepened my own, and I became more and more touched by the stories they told. When I felt awkward in the beginning, they didn't seem to care. And when I thought I was getting better at engaging with them, they weren't particularly impressed. When I could finally be myself with these sweet people, they gave me everything they had—the gift of their untold stories.

For all who were able to attend, I offered a prayer service in the community room. We gathered there to pray and share our stories around a large, round table where wheelchairs fit comfortably. I would read chapters from *Chicken Soup for the Soul;* the patients seemed to like the stories' simplicity and sensitivity. And we had some interesting events! One morning, an elderly lady who was usually incoherent seemed to be sleeping through the service. Suddenly, she woke up and sang—word for word—the first verse of "Amazing Grace"! Often, patients would ask me if God had forgotten them and then begin to cry. I would then see some not-so-able soul reach a shaking hand over to that person for comfort. We would end our services by thanking God for things we were grateful for. Each time, I was amazed that these people, who had lost almost everything and lived diverse lives, were able to find grace in living another day—and a sense of community with one another.

One day, I knocked on the closed door of a patient's room. A woman opened it a crack and said hello to me. I told her I was the chaplain and asked if she'd like me to stop by for a while. She said, "Oh, thank you for offering, but I have to have my hair done. Maybe some other time you could come by." I told her I'd be happy to come back another day. When I returned for my next shift, I found out the woman had died that night.

The floor usually housed several AIDS patients at a given time. One woman told the story of how her boyfriend had called her from South Carolina and informed her that he had AIDS. "The minute I heard him say that," she told me, "I knew I was gonna have it." She was in her early thirties and had young children. She talked about how hard it was to leave them. She would greet me with a smile and make sure she was presentable, as though I were a visitor. As she got weaker and weaker, she would whisper to me that it was very, very hard to die from AIDS.

A man I met in the long-term care unit suffered from multiple sclerosis. He could hardly move his body. I'd go in and say hello, and he'd smile back at me—but he never seemed to want to engage in conversation.

One day, he motioned for me to stay. He turned his head towards a table and motioned for me to bring over a box on his side table.

I brought over the shoe box, and he had me open it. Inside were pictures of him as a young, healthy, married man with his family. He had clippings about owning his own business —how he'd helped build his church and had been a leader in town government. He had pictures of his parents and grandchildren. He smiled proudly as I looked at each of them.

When a nurse entered the room to give him his medication, I put the pictures away. I thought: *Here is a man who has lost so much; his life history is reduced to pictures in a box. I feel graced by the honor of his invitation to share a glimpse into his life.*

One patient I visited regularly was Ann, and during a meeting with the staff, I was asked to speak to her about the very real possibility of her dying within a few months. I was surprised that the staff had never broached this with Ann. They said they were frustrated with her oncology doctor, because he never told her outright that she most likely would die from her recurrence of breast cancer. They felt that she was dealing with a lot of stress by trying to "get better" in order to go home, when they knew she'd most likely never leave the hospital alive.

Ann was in her late thirties. A divorced woman, she had a devoted boyfriend and a teenaged son, as well as many, many friends who visited her regularly. She was always happy to see me and greeted me with her great smile and soft voice. "Oh, Kris, I've really missed you!" she'd tell me. Then she'd jump right into the stories and events that had taken place since our last time together.

Ann's cancer had spread throughout her body and into her brain. Her body had ballooned, and she needed a large hoist to lift her out of bed. She would share with me how painful it was to be manipulated that way. She talked about her plans to go home and how she couldn't wait to get out of the hospital.

One day, I asked her if she had ever considered that she might not be able to leave the hospital and go home. She stared at me for a long time, not saying anything.

I waited a while and then asked again how she would feel if that was the case.

"I would feel very, very disappointed!" she said with deep intensity. Then she looked down at her hands and cried. I put my arms around her. We held each other. I had tears in my eyes. She didn't want to talk anymore.

Several visits later, the moment seemed right again to bring up the subject of Ann not leaving the hospital. "Ann," I asked her, "if you aren't able to leave the hospital, would you like to say a few words to your family and friends, maybe in a letter, about how you feel about them?"

She brightened up and said without hesitation, "Oh, Kris, I'd love to do that, but I can't write well anymore."

I told her that she could dictate what she wanted to say, and I'd write it out for her.

"That would be wonderful!" she told me. We began by making a list of all the family and friends who had been there for her throughout her long hospital stay. I think we had fifteen names in all.

We began with her son. She told him she loved him and thanked him for being such a great boy. And then she just kept going through the list of people. I took the dictation home, typed it out in big print, and brought it back to her. She was thrilled. She spent days telling me the corrections and additions I needed to make, and by the time we were done, it seemed Ann had created a book of remembrances. I told her I'd be happy to give the book to her family when the time came.

She completely surprised me by saying, "I don't want to wait for my family and friends to hear how I feel about them. I want to read this to them now, while I'm still here. Do you think that's possible, Kris?"

I spoke to the nursing staff. They were so happy that Ann seemed to be active in her dying process. They promised to help us however they could. Ann called each and every person on her list and asked them to come to the hospital on the designated day, saying she had something she wanted to tell them. Ann had many visitors who acted happy and bubbly, not wishing to upset her in any way. But the reality was that Ann could never be herself, because she was worried that her visitors would be upset if she told them about her pain and fear of dying.

On the designated morning, Ann's family and friends came, looking scared themselves about what Ann was going to say to them. We had the laundry room to ourselves for privacy. There we were, all tucked into a very small space. Ann, in her wheelchair in the center of the room, looked at everybody and thanked them for coming before she started to read.

Within two words, everyone in the room was crying. Nobody could stop. But Ann carried on. She would look at the person she wanted to talk to, and when she finished, she would turn her head to the next one. It was as though she had given them the gift of truth, and now they could breathe. Their smiles were no longer forced. They thanked and hugged her, and at last, she could cry in front of them.

Several months later, I received a call at home telling me that Ann was nearing death. Would I come in and be with the family? I drove down to the hospital, thinking what a gift this courageous woman had been to me. I raced to her room where I found her surrounded by her loved ones. They beckoned me to come closer, and I held Ann's hand. We had talked about this moment for more than a year, and somehow, I felt proud of her willingness to finally go. She had suffered so much. There was a rattling sound to her breathing, and then, suddenly, she just didn't exhale. Everything became quiet. We all looked at her, as though not quite believing that, after all this time, she was actually gone.

I was asked to speak at her funeral Mass and attend the reception that followed. Ann's sister gave me a memento that Ann wanted me to have—a framed picture of her. I couldn't believe that the pretty, thin girl looking back at me was Ann. What was the same, however, which I will always remember, was the beautiful smile that radiated so much love.

CHAPTER 9
GIVING UP SECRETS

Over time, I began to find strength through my pastoral training. I became a very good observer and had insight into my patients' feelings. My supervisor at the time was Sister Dorothy, from the hospital where I'd had my first clinical-pastoral placement. Within the CPE group, my voice grew as I was willing to share my feelings, and I developed leadership qualities in the group's dynamics.

My writing, too, was praised, and I enjoyed creating prayer and meditation services. In the middle of my second unit of CPE, I needed to write a reflective piece about some unresolved issue. Then it hit me: I had run out of things to say! I had exhausted the options in writing about experiences I was comfortable sharing. I would have to think of something new.

For the first time, I considered writing about having given up a child for adoption. Just thinking about it made me break out in hives. Other than Larry and my friend Alberta, I hadn't told anyone. They had gotten me through years of birthdays and holidays, when I'd been wondering about Kyra.

I wrote the paper. I don't remember exactly what I said. Just the basic facts, I think. I was shaking when I finished it. On the day when I turned it in to Sister Dorothy, I could hardly breathe.

That evening, I attended a didactic session in which a woman talked about her work at a halfway house. She helped women who had no other place to live and care for their babies. She was so genuine, so authentic and sincere, that my already cracking psyche cracked open even more. In that moment, I felt as though I had never been a real person, ever, in my life—that I'd been a fraud. Waves of pain rolled over me again and again. I could hardly walk to my car.

I told Larry I had written the paper about Kyra. He was worried. "Why upset yourself? You've been doing fine all these years. Why talk about it now?" he asked. I knew he wanted to protect me, but I couldn't hold up the wall of secrets anymore.

The next time I saw Sister Dorothy, her kindness melted me. She asked, "Have you forgiven yourself, Kris?" Forgiven myself! How could I do that? I had no idea, no idea at all, how that was possible. I hadn't realized the weight of guilt and shame I was carrying.

Months passed before I felt safe enough to share my story with my CPE group. It was a tremendous challenge for me to trust other people. The day I shared my story, a man in the group told us how he'd been adopted, and that he'd never thought about how hard it might have been for his birth mother to give him up. A woman shared about being an adoptive mother, and about her doubts over being a good mother. There we were—birth mother, adopted son, and adoptive mother—all in the same room, in the same story.

After sharing my story, I had a dream. In the dream, I was in a room of a house without walls; only studs crisscrossed the rooms. There were many people milling about. I was looking through a room to the outside, and what I saw looking back at me was a polar bear. I was amazed at the size and whiteness of this bear. It followed me as I moved from one end of the room to the other. I wondered if it was safe for me to go outside.

I shared my dream at CPE, and it was met with great excitement. I hadn't done any work with dreams before, so I had no idea that mine was considered a BIG dream— one that might indicate that walls of shame and guilt were melting away. Maybe the glacier that held all of the denial of the repressed feelings and pain I was in had shifted. And maybe the power of such a creature lived in me! Was it possible I was coming out of hibernation…where all of my emotions had slept for so many years…and now I could look inward at myself? If I was the bear and the bear was me, then I had a mighty force to reckon with…and a wild… huge voice to let loose.

I decided to search for my brother, Howard. I hadn't seen him in more than forty years. I had talked and written CPE papers about him. My heart ached for him. Many years before, when Larry and I had first married, Larry called the institution where my brother was, on my behalf. He asked the administrator if Howard would know me if I visited him on a regular basis. "No," was the answer Larry got. It seemed easier to accept that answer than to search any further into my brother's condition, so I had left it at that. I was used to leaving things where they landed. But now I was opening up about how I had felt when my mother told me never to say that I had a brother.

My one memory of him is so old. In the memory, I climbed into the back seat of a car, and as I got adjusted, an adult was closing the car door. I said, "Where's Howie?" The adult told me that Howie couldn't come with us. I remember feeling very sad about this and looking at Howie through the car window as we pulled away.

Now, decades later, I needed to see him again.

I found him living in a state-run institution south of Boston. It was a campus with many large administrative buildings. Clients resided in smaller quarters that offered a dining area, recreation space, and bedrooms accommodating four people. He'd been there since he was five years old. His records showed he had two living sisters. It also showed that he hadn't been visited in decades. The administrative staff, as well as the doctors, were amazed to hear from me after so many years. They wanted to meet with me before I saw Howie.

My friend Ann, a school psychologist, came with me. This was fortunate, because I completely lost my voice the day before the meeting. Ann had to do all the questioning and answering for me. They had never had a case quite like mine: a relative coming out of the woodwork, so many years later. They wanted to know what my intentions were. I said I wanted closure.

They brought me to his room, which he shared with several other men. I was told he could dress and feed himself and had been trained to do simple tasks. I turned around and saw knees coming towards me. They were my knees, kind of square, and it was those knees that made me cry. Who knew that we would share resemblance? *He was my brother.* There he was, still looking like a boy in his striped shirt and Bermuda shorts and sneakers.

We were brought into a room together. I gave Howie some candy that I'd been told he liked. He had the face of someone who had been institutionalized all his life. He didn't speak, although I was told he could say some words. I just stared at him. I felt very emotional and awkward. I could see our mother's face stamped on him. I felt connected to him, somehow. It was amazing to see our physical similarities. It made our lives together real. I could say I had a brother.

The state-run facility has been drastically reduced since my first meeting with Howie. The state now mandates that all clients who can be introduced into community must be housed in group homes. Howie falls into a category of clients deemed unable to thrive in that setting. He now lives in a home with several other men who also need close attention and monitoring. It's located on the edge of the property that once belonged to the larger facility. It was decided that this was best, because the clients were familiar with the area and the setting wasn't near any residential neighborhoods. Recently, I received a letter from his staff informing me that they had installed an alarm in the house to alert them when he wandered off. Evidently, he is notorious for bounding out the door to go for walks.

My visits to Howie since that first day have been filled with longing to have known him better. The staff at his home appears to genuinely care for him, and that settles my heart. I remember a book called *The Clowns of God*. It was about the innocence of the developmentally challenged and how their gift to the world is to make God smile. That's Howie's gift, too. I am grateful to be a recipient.

CHAPTER 10
CERTIFICATION

Applying for certification to become a Catholic chaplain requires a tremendous amount of work. It requires not only four completed units of CPE, but also hundreds of pages of questions—or so it seems—requiring answers that demonstrate the knowledge and ability to fulfill your chaplaincy duties.

I threw myself into the task and spent my third and fourth units of CPE diligently fulfilling whatever was asked of me in order to complete the process. I was self-confident and believed that when I appeared before the Certification Committee, I'd be able to demonstrate my personal, pastoral, professional, and theological competencies, both orally and in writing.

The day arrived for me to appear before the committee in Rhode Island. I felt nervous and excited. I traveled with one of my classmates, who was also being interviewed. Another classmate traveled separately, and a dear friend met me there to lend support. We all were to appear before different teams. Each team had received copies of our completed work and prepared questions for us.

I was invited into a room where two nuns and one female minister greeted me. The team chairperson was a nun in her late sixties. She smiled at me and read the report she had written about my work. When she'd finished, I realized that, in essence, she thought my materials were too good to be true. She smiled my way again, and asked, "Kris, why is it that you seem to need to be so good?"

I didn't know what to say. I started to feel not very good at all. I replied that I had done the best job I could.

"Hmmmm," was the sound that came from her. She continued, "Tell us about your theology, about your relationship with God."

I stated that what was exciting for me was the realization of the feminine face of God; that during my theological studies, I had realized the Church's patriarchal view of the experience of God was beginning to shift; that there seemed to be a new awakening of the more nurturing and feminine aspects of the experience of the Spirit.

"Well," she said, "why don't we just do some role playing and see how well you do at that?!" Her tone was condescending and strident, and I felt as though she was mocking me. She began, "I'll be a girl in the hospital who's pregnant and wondering if she should keep her baby or have an abortion, and you'll be the chaplain."

I was taken aback by the scenario she had chosen. But in a calm voice I introduced myself as the chaplain. I asked if she would like to talk about her situation.

With that, she started to holler. Whenever I tried to speak, she would scream louder, and in the role-playing, she ordered me out of her room.

I was shocked and pretty much speechless. I had worked with patients for four years, and no one had ever behaved that way. And if anyone had reacted as she was doing, I know I would have become very quiet in order to help calm the situation. I knew things were not going well at all.

With disgust in her voice, the nun informed me the interview was over, and I should wait in the outer room!

Devastated, I knew I didn't pass whatever that test was about.

My friend Paula was waiting for me. She looked at me and couldn't believe the expression on my face. "Oh my God," she gasped. "What happened to you?"

I couldn't speak. Several minutes later, I was called back to the interview room, and the chairperson informed me that I would not be recommended for certification. "Clearly, you are nothing like what your documents have portrayed you to be, and obviously you can't deal with a patient in crisis!" she proclaimed. "Also," she continued, "it is strongly recommended that you begin theological studies somewhere, because you have no real theology!"

At the time, I had been assisting the CPE staff in Western Massachusetts in any way they could use me. I also had been attending Boston College, working on a master's degree that included a good deal of theological study. I looked around the table at each person, but there wasn't much I felt I could say. However, as I gathered my materials, I looked at the team leader and said, "I am quite sure I have a theology." With that, I left the room.

I was the only one in my peer group who did not receive a recommendation. I felt absolutely crushed. The ride home was horrible. When I walked into my house, the telephone was ringing. It was Larry. I bawled like a baby. Friends kept calling to congratulate me, and I had to tell them what had happened. No one could believe that I hadn't been certified. I cried myself to sleep that night—something I hadn't done since I was a child.

When I returned for the next CPE day, I still felt humiliated. I had put everything I had into the chaplaincy process and felt as though I had failed. However, I was met by my teachers and peers with respect, love, and honor, and I was given much encouragement to try again.

I learned that the chairperson of my certification committee had a reputation for intimidating applicants, scaring even grown men into delaying six months more to apply for certification rather than risk having her as their team leader. I hadn't known any of this. I was informed that her behavior towards me was noted by another member on that committee and reported to the regional committee. Despite knowing that she had this reputation, I still felt crushed. It took time for my wounded heart to heal and feel the excitement I had felt before my interview.

Slowly, I began to feel like my old self again. Six months later, after reapplication, I appeared before another committee. Before I was asked to speak, the chairperson offered me a genuinely sincere apology for how I had been treated by the first chairperson. I was complimented by the other team members on the excellence of my written materials and was able to answer all of their questions in an appropriate way. When I left, I was assured that their recommendation for my certification would be forwarded to the national committee.

The ending was happy, but because of that experience, something had happened to me on the deepest level. Ultimately, one of the most painful episodes in my life— failing to pass my certification attempt—would be the key to opening myself to the experience of soul. As a result, I now look upon that first team leader with gratitude and love. She was the blessing and the curse that changed my life. It was to be some time, however, before I could see it that way.

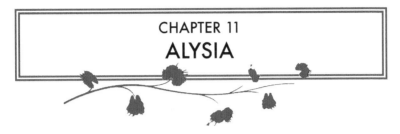

CHAPTER 11
ALYSIA

Several months after the certification rejection, I experienced recurring pain in my back. I felt so tense and tight. Massage therapy helped, but not for long. I felt that if I went to a doctor, I would most likely be given a muscle relaxant or pain killers, and I didn't want to go that route.

For more than a year, I had been carrying a card in my wallet with the name and number of an energy healer named Alysia Tromblay. A fellow CPE student had seen her after a foot injury, and told me about her amazing results. I had absolutely no idea what an energy healer did; but I felt miserable, so I decided to make an appointment.

I don't know what I expected, but I was surprised when Alysia turned out to be an extraordinarily beautiful woman in her thirties—fair-skinned with long blonde hair, blue eyes, and a slender body. She dressed in beautifully flowing clothes and had a smile so inviting that it melted away whatever my heavy heart was carrying. In her studio, incense filled the air. I was intrigued by many new and interesting things in the room: drums, feathers, and a statue of an Asian woman on top of a lotus, holding children in her arms.

She asked me why I had come to see her.

I told her my wails and woes about not having been certified as a chaplain; about the unkindness of the chairperson who had told me I just couldn't be *that* good; about how I had said I thought the feminine face of God was a good theology. But, I concluded, what I was really there for was a throbbing pain in my back that wouldn't go away. "Could you help me with that?" I asked her.

Alysia just smiled at me. She asked, "Kris, do you like being a victim?"

"A victim!" I cried. I could feel my face and neck get red. "But she committed an injustice towards me," I informed her. "She was wrong, and I was right to feel hurt!"

Alysia smiled and said softly, "Kris, do you think she could have touched that spot in you if you hadn't been trying to be so good?"

I didn't know what to say.

"It seems to me," she continued, "that you have probably been trying to be good all your life, and finally this event smacked you between the eyes. Maybe that's what we should look at."

I felt completely confused. What did my drive to be good have to do with the pain in my back?

"Kris," she said, "maybe this issue finally got big enough for you to see it. Maybe it's sitting on your back!"

I left her studio reeling. This woman had just put the responsibility of all that had happened in my lap.

"Everything is connected," she told me, "so the incident with the chairperson has everything to do with your stuff."

When I shared this with my friend, Paula, she thought it was ridiculous. "You were unjustly treated. How could it be your fault?" she demanded. I was lucky to have such a faithful friend.

And yet, this visit to Alysia marked the beginning of seeing, hearing, and thinking in a new way—a way that asked me to tell the truth about myself, my life, and my relationship to others. I came to learn that everything I said had a consequence, and it would be better to awaken to this truth than to be asleep, as I had been up until that time. I experienced the beginning of waking up and knowing who I was.

Working with Alysia expanded my awareness of soul, *my soul*. My heart had been cracked open in CPE. Now, through the continual broadening of my heart's opening, I was hearing the sound of my soul for the first time.

Several weeks into seeing Alysia, she smiled at me and said, "Kris, did you really think you could tell a nun of more than fifty years, who had been trained in pre-Vatican II days, that your theology was based on the feminine face of God?"

I burst out laughing. Put to me that way, and even I could hear how ridiculous that must have sounded to her.

Alysia continued, "Did you ever consider you might be a threat to her? You're well-groomed, well-dressed, and obviously intelligent. Maybe your feminine face is the one who will replace the face she has known all of her religious life."

I had never thought of that possibility. Laity were filling many roles that the clergy, until now, had filled.

"Kris, you need to be more aware of your effect," she told me.

It had never really crossed my mind—but it was clearly high time that I learned that I do have an effect on people.

CHAPTER 12
WHAT DO YOU DO WHEN A LAMA COMES TO TOWN?

Alysia was raised in the Egyptian Coptic Church. Her exposure to the nature of the mind and soul, sound and energy healing began as a child under the teachings of Egyptian Fakir Master Hamid Bey. In the eighties, she met Reverend Rosalyn Bruyere, author of *Wheels of Light*, and studied the healing arts with her extensively. For many years, Alysia maintained a practice in New York City and Northampton, Massachusetts, where I met her. In 1991, she first traveled to the Menri Monastery in India to meet the H.H. 33rd Menri Trizin, Lungtok Tempai Nyima, leader of the Bön people, the indigenous people of Tibet. As a result of that meeting, she formed a lifelong commitment to the preservation of the Bön people and their spiritual traditions. Later, her love of the voice and its power for healing led her to meet and work with Jill Purce, author of *The Mystic Spiral: Journey of the Soul*. Alysia says that it is through that work that she found the power of the group chant.

Alysia was very different from the teachers I had known in the past. Although my heart had been cracked open during my chaplaincy training, Alysia's method or style of counseling was so penetrating and incisive that I had no place to hide. She scared me a little, but when I would have an "Aha!" moment with her, my feelings were so extraordinary that I kept going back for more and more.

One day, at the end of a session with Alysia, she asked me, "What do you do when a lama comes to town?"

I had no idea. Another client she posed that question to thought she was literally housing llamas in her back yard for the weekend. We roared with laughter at the thought of it. Instead, we learned that His Holiness, leader of the Bön people, was coming to our area to give a retreat. I was fascinated and decided to attend the teachings. Deeply moved by the ceremonies I witnessed, I became interested in learning more about the indigenous people of Tibet.

In 1959, His Holiness was living at Drepung Monastery in Lhasa, Tibet, when the Chinese takeover forced him to flee, on foot, to Nepal. He carried on the backs of mules the sacred texts and woodblocks of the Bön religion and culture, and managed to get to New Delhi, India, to have them preserved. Today, Menri Monastery—named for the original, now destroyed, Menri Monastery in the Tsang region of Tibet—is the current spiritual and administrative center for all Bönpo in exile. Adjacent to the monastery is a Bön community comprised of living facilities for children, a school, a health center, and the village of Dolanji. Living in the Hostel for Menri Children are boys whose families have placed them in the care of the monastery for their upbringing and religious training. The Bön Children's Home houses girls and boys, sent sometimes from great distances by families who want their children to have a traditional as well as secular education. All of the children attend the Central School for Tibetans, where they receive a modern education through tenth grade in the context of Bön teachings, traditions, and culture.

Alysia shared many stories about her visits to the monastery, being in the company of His Holiness and the lamas, and the effect that the orphans had upon her. It all sounded so intriguing that I wondered if I might go to the monastery someday myself.

There is no adequate way to describe the kind of intensive, loving work that Alysia does.

I wanted to love in the intentional way that she loved. It took me years to sense that kind of spiritual depth and call it my own. During the journey to awareness of my soul, Alysia poked, prodded, assailed, and confronted all that was asleep in me, and demanded that it awaken.

I can remember realizing that when I was asked a question, my first instinct was to think that I didn't know the answer, or wonder what the right answer was. I hadn't realized that my childhood of secrets had left its mark on my ability to speak the truth. Those early traumas had adulterated my ability to tell my story. My true story had become silenced. I was beginning to understand that although I couldn't erase the mark of my childhood experiences, I could transform the energy around it. I had to stay aware of my ability to obscure truth; it was deeply ingrained in me. I needed to understand what had been burned into the hard drive of my mind. My practice would be to ferret out all the places that weren't sure or that might seek the easier thing to do. I had to confront my unconscious pattern of keeping my truth asleep. "Which did I serve?" I had to ask myself, and understand that I had thirty-three years of secrets weighed against a few months of truth-telling. The secrets in my mind could try to trap my soul's light, if I didn't demand their truthful counterparts to show themselves.

My mind was exploding with excitement over my new discoveries. One evening while at dinner with Larry, I told him about an amazing discovery I had made that day during a session with Alysia. "Do you know," I said, "that I've always lived in my ego as though that's who I am—the voice inside constantly striving to achieve, acquire, and identify with things that never satisfy? Since my heart has been opening, I've realized I am Spirit living in a human body filled with yearning to be me—without the chase or separation from God. I can now tell my ego: Thank you very much for all the help you have given me to survive, but you can rest now."

He just looked at me and stared.

"Do you understand anything I've just said?" I asked him.

"Not a word!" he replied.

I couldn't stop talking about this newfound discovery within myself. It changed everything. I felt thrilled to be alive.

Strange as it seems, I never brought up with Alysia the fact that I had given my baby up for adoption, although I had been seeing her for more than a year.

One night, Larry and I went to see "Secrets and Lies," a movie about an adopted daughter finding her birth mother. As the daughter and birth mother met, and the birth mother decided to introduce the daughter to her family, I felt my body begin to heave; I bit my lips and dug my nails into my hands, trying not to sob in the theater. When the movie was over, I had to walk around the parking lot for many minutes to regain my composure. Larry took me to dinner, and we shared a bottle of wine. All I could talk about was the movie. I couldn't imagine meeting my daughter, let alone introducing her to my family.

The next morning, I awoke with a horrendous sinus inflammation. "That was fast!" I thought. I began to realize the effort it had cost me at the theater to hold in my emotions. My body's response was to get sick with an infection in my head and throat—the throat that had been unable to speak truth for so long.

I walked into Alysia's studio and proclaimed, "I know why I get sinus infections so many times a year and need antibiotics so often."

Alysia was astonished I had left out that piece of information about myself. I was just excited to experience the body-mind connection of emotions to illness. It wasn't theory anymore. Alysia gently invited me to talk about my experience. I told her about sharing my story at CPE, and that I'd felt better for doing that.

"Have you considered finding your daughter?" she asked.

"No," I answered. "I haven't."

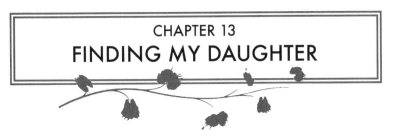

CHAPTER 13
FINDING MY DAUGHTER

"Why haven't you thought about finding your child?" Alysia asked me.

"I thought I should leave well enough alone," I told her. "I signed the release papers for Kyra's adoption, and I've thought part of the agreement has been to stay out of her life." Just talking about the possibility of finding my daughter caused my neck to get red and blotchy, sometimes bumpy, with instant hives.

"Don't you think you have the right to know about her well-being?" she asked me.

"I've never thought I had any rights," I confessed.

The truth was I had wondered about searching for Kyra since the day I had given her up. Whenever I thought about the possibility of finding her, I felt overwhelmed with emotion and would push the desire away. Here I was being challenged to think heretical thoughts: As a birth mother, I had the right, at least in some states, to initiate a search for my daughter, and now, for the first time, to think about the possibility that my birth daughter might be looking for me.

I shared with Larry what Alysia and I had talked about.

"What would you do if you found her?" he wanted to know. "How would this change our lives? After all, Joan and Michael don't even know about Kyra."

Larry wasn't at all sure that looking for my daughter was such a good idea, but I had kept my secret bottled up for thirty-three years, and it felt like I'd burst if I didn't let it out.

I couldn't remember the name of the adoption agency I had gone through those many years ago. I began calling state agencies that helped women search for their adopted-out children, but they couldn't help, because I had used a private agency. After several calls, a nameless woman at the other end of the telephone line said to me, "Sister, you go find your baby!" Having said that, she gave me a number to call, which led me to the name of the adoption agency in southern Connecticut. The process took many weeks. Each time I'd dial a number, my body would seize with fear. I couldn't stand up. During one call, I actually slid to the floor. Every time I asked a question, I was revealing that I was a birth mother. I had never spoken publicly before about my secret, and now I was announcing it to perfect strangers.

I made contact with the Connecticut adoption agency, and they sent me forms to fill out. They'd do a search for one month for a certain fee, and if that failed, I would have to pay an additional sum of money.

The fee hardly seemed important compared to the dilemma I faced about telling Joan and Michael. If I told them now about Kyra and about the instituted search, then we could all hope and wait together for some news. If I was reunited with Kyra and hadn't told Joan and Michael, then they would hear about her birth and, by the way, "Here's your sister."

This was quite the dilemma for me. I was filled with feelings of excitement and dread: excitement because I was doing something to find my daughter; dread because I didn't know how my children would feel after discovering they had a sister of whom they hadn't known. I felt very vulnerable about revealing a secret that had left me feeling shame and guilt for so long.

I liked the first plan. Larry liked the second one, because he didn't think there was much hope of ever finding her. He said, "Why cause so much commotion in our family?"

I went with my instincts. It was very hard to go against Larry's wishes. He was silent, and I knew he was worried. It was the first time I said to him: "You have two children; I have three."

I don't know if Joan or Michael kept the letter I wrote telling them about having had a baby as a teenager and giving her up for adoption. I do know that Larry and I have two incredible children. After reading the letter, Joan and Michael were compassionate and understanding. "We can't believe what a taboo you had to live with," they said. "It's like you lived in the Dark Ages!" Their experience as teenagers was very different from mine, fortunately.

It was a Thursday when we shared the story of Kyra with Joan and Michael. The following Monday evening, while staying at my friend Paula's apartment in Boston, I received a message from Larry. A woman from the adoption agency wanted me to call her.

"Oh God," I thought. "This couldn't have happened already!"

The woman at the agency had made contact with Kyra. I was informed that she lived in Connecticut, had a son, was a licensed practical nurse, and very much wanted to hear from me. She had registered years before, signifying she was willing to meet her birth mother. I was given her telephone number and the time to call her the following day. My head was spinning. My heart was pounding.

I can't adequately describe the experience of dialing Kyra's telephone number and hearing her voice on the other end of the line. "Hello, Kyra," I began. I could hardly recognize my own voice…I sounded so nervous. This was the moment I had dreamed about, and it was happening. My mind was spinning. It was all I could do not to burst into tears of joy and release. My dream had become real!

She interrupted me. "Before you say anything," she said, "I want you to know that I have had a beautiful life, and I want to thank you for having me. I can't imagine what it was like to be a teenager giving birth to a baby and to have no way to care for it! I think of the day you pushed me out and the pain you must have been in."

Her words astonished me. My tension eased a bit. I was thrilled, and a bit surprised, that we were starting our reunion from such a positive place. She told me she had a son named Phillip, whom she adored. "He's the love of my life."

I was overcome. I didn't know what to say. I was amazed we were talking to each other. She told me she'd registered to find me when she was nineteen, but hadn't told her parents or siblings. She spoke about having an older sister and younger brother. Her voice sounded excited. She asked about my life. "Do you have children? She was fascinated when I told her about Joan and Michael. "I've never known anyone who was my blood relative," she told me. "I can't imagine having a sister and brother who are actually related to me." We exchanged addresses. She said she'd send me a picture of herself, and that she'd call me very soon. Every day, for many, many months, I walked to the mailbox to see if Kyra had written. There was nothing from her in the mailbox. But in that initial thrill of having made contact with my daughter, I could have flown just by lifting my arms. The impossible had happened.

I couldn't contain myself. I told my sister, Beverly. She had never suspected why I had been away in New York City for six months those many years ago. I wrote to close relatives to tell them my secret. I called my friends and met them for lunch to share about this unspoken part of my life. I told them how I'd always felt as though they had never known the real me because of what I'd kept secret. One of my dearest friends, Paddy, has a daughter whose birthday is the same as Kyra's. I could finally tell her that wishing her daughter happy birthday on December 27 had meant so much to me all through the years.

I had opened my life for this new daughter to come in, but she was very, very silent. I learned that I'd expected too much of her. She, too, had her secrets. She hadn't been able to tell her parents about wanting to find me. She had also shared in our visit that she hadn't done any counseling work to sort out her feelings about searching for her birth mother. But I was used to waiting. I could wait some more.

Alysia suggested I attend a workshop given by a woman named Jill Purce. It was called the Healing Voice workshop, in Devon, England. I packed my bag for a very long journey—a journey that would change my life.

CHAPTER 14
JILL PURCE

I was excited to be traveling to Europe for the first time. I went with several other participants—people who were also doing healing work with Alysia. By the time I arrived in Devon, I was absolutely exhausted from hauling a ridiculously overstuffed duffel bag through train stations, as we traveled down the coast of England. My companions were considerably younger than I was and thought everything we encountered was a great adventure. However, by the time we arrived at the retreat house, I was ready to pack it up and return home. I hadn't even finished registering when I felt as though I had used up all my physical reserves. Being home with Larry in my own bed was all I could think about. I realized I had absolutely no idea what I had signed up for.

Jill Purce's work is nothing less than profound. She believes that our families and ancestors are resonant fields, and the most effective way of healing them is through resonance and the voice in the context of ceremony. She works ceremonially with the resonant fields of family, revealing the dynamic of their patterns to restore love and order. Specifically, through ceremonies, chanting, and explorations with sound for healing and transformation of consciousness, Jill somehow weaves the attending group through the psycho-physical effects of breathing, chanting, and meditation. In our workshop, we learned how to tone and listen together, moving from the intuitive level into meditative states. The power of this process hit me like a ton of bricks.

I walked around in what felt like an altered state for most of the week, as I took in the incredible meaning of what was being presented. If what Jill was saying was true, then I was experiencing the resonant field of my lineage: my mother and father! Oh no!

My mother was devastated by illness and depression throughout her life. What on earth had she had to carry all those years? Her own mother had died of consumption at forty-seven, her father of heart failure at forty-six. I'd never known my father, but I knew that his mother had a nervous breakdown in her twenties. This left my father to be raised by his not-so-nurturing father, a musician who died of a heart attack in his forties. My lineage was frightening at best. Was I carrying this field of despair, sadness, and illness around with me?

My cousin had once told me an amazing story. My grandmother, Margaret, had come to America when she was sixteen years old and lived with her sister and her sister's husband. She became pregnant by her sister's husband and had a baby boy, who was raised by her sister and brother-in-law as their own. My cousin learned this story from that boy's daughters. The larger family, however, continued to keep it a secret. If this is true, it means that my grandmother had a baby out of wedlock and kept it a secret.

Margaret went on to marry and have four more children, the youngest of whom was my mother, Dorothy. Dorothy's son, my brother Howard, was severely mentally challenged, and she relinquished custody to the Commonwealth of Massachusetts. She kept this secret and raised me to keep the secret, too. Then I got pregnant at age eighteen and gave the baby up for adoption. I had my own secret to keep.

My grandmother was dead at forty-seven, my mother at sixty. I had suffered for years with sinus infection after sinus infection, leaving me miserable in bed for days. The thought was awakening in me that, by holding these secrets in the lineage, we only perpetuated the events that called for secrets to repeat themselves. I hoped that, simply by telling the truth, I could possibly heal this fissure in my lineage.

The group gathered each day to share their experiences as their feelings and emotions were being tapped. I decided to share my story of secrets and lies. I had come to believe that giving up a child was the most unnatural act a woman could commit. I don't know what I thought would happen by revealing what, to me, had been the worst secret imaginable. I told them that I could not imagine being on the other side of the pain I felt for having given up my child. When I sat down, I sobbed and sobbed. I was staggered by my own feelings of judgment and shame. However, I was held and comforted by many loving arms.

Other people shared their stories, and I realized I was feeling their pain, too. It seemed that pain was pain, after all. My pain wasn't greater than anyone else's. I had lived most of my days believing my pain was greater than other people's, which had kept me separated and detached. I saw that I'd always held my pain, ready for someone to notice that my life had been difficult as a child and tell me that it was amazing I had survived. I had always felt desperate for someone—anyone—to nurture me. If I could let this pain go, then I wouldn't need to be a victim anymore. This could mean freedom for me!

At breakfast one morning, the dining hall was packed. I sat at a table filled with people. The woman across from me said, "I don't know what I'm going to do when I get home. How will I ever explain this experience to my family and friends?"

"I know how you feel," I said, tears welling up. My chest began to heave, and a sound I'd never made before came out of me. I couldn't stop the wail until it had reached its end. I heard chairs moving and dishes being dropped as people hurriedly left the room. But I couldn't stop screaming. I was alone at my table when a beautiful woman named Claire came and surrounded me with her arms. She rocked me, caressed my face, and said, "You'll be all right now. You are very brave."

Sofie, a young woman I had met the day before, also came to me. She leaned closer to me and said, "Kris, I never knew a birth mother could feel what I have just witnessed come out of you. I had no idea the pain involved in giving up a baby. For the first time, I can imagine what it was like for my birth mother to give me away." I thanked her for sharing that with me.

Something very big was happening to me. I was crying and feeling happy at the same time. The heaviness on my heart was being lifted. I was no longer the bearer of secrets in my family. I felt as though I was appearing before people as I really was for the first time. Being surrounded by a unified field of love, a force larger than pain and suffering, beckoned my soul to come forward. The whole of me, the soul of me, was larger than the sum of its parts. I came to realize that there was more to me than the pain I bore.

CHAPTER 15
MOTHER LIONS

Every day of the workshop had its own format, loosely guided by the energy of the group. Jill's skill at weaving each day's evolution into deeper spiritual meaning and creating openings for sharing led the group to greater trust and expressions of hope and healing.

I found each day filled with the unknown. My mind would endlessly look for answers to questions floating in my head: *What is Jill doing now? How long will this segment last? Is Jill going to make that long-winded person stop talking? When do they eat lunch in England?*

As time went on, my mind seemed to ease up on the questions. I began simply to be in the moment, allowing myself to experience whatever was coming up next. I began to see that the agitation I felt as I listened to people telling their endless stories was more about me than it was about them. In fact, these urges brought up my impatience, judgment, and need to know and control what would happen every minute.

One day, Jill gathered us in the chapel. Eighty to a one hundred of us were assembled, some in chairs along the back wall, but most of us on cushions on the floor. "Today," Jill announced, "we're going to do mother lions!"

She had taken us through many meditations throughout the week, but I had never heard of a meditation called mother lions! She began taking us through the process of preparing to go deeply into our beings, inviting us to expect a vision to come forward. My mind was twisting itself into some understanding about what was being instructed.

Jill was taking us into strange territory—her instructions sounded as foreign to me as her British accent. As she continued, she told us we would be doing a meditation the next day about father lines. "Oh!" This time I heard her clearly: She had said mother *lines*, not mother lions!

We were instructed to call our mother's name and envision, if we could, our mother coming forward into that vision. We were then to greet her with love and gratitude, bearing gifts for her. We were to invite her to put all the guilt, anger, and suffering we had experienced into a basket and burn it, bury it, or sail it down the river, and celebrate the release of all that had hindered our relationship. After doing this with our mother, we would then call our grandmother's name and proceed again with the same process, and on again down the line of our mother's lineage. If we didn't have a name to use, we could simply say *mother*. Jill suggested we share our experience with the person beside us when the meditation ended.

I felt nervous about the meditation and even more nervous about sharing. I didn't know what to expect, but I was amazed at how deep my trance state could go. My whole body seemed to resonate with a tingling vibration. If nothing else, I felt very serene. I began to call my mother's name: Dorothy, Dorothy, Dorothy. And then I had a vision, a vision of beautiful bluebell flowers! They were everywhere. But no mother appeared to me. I didn't know if I should just skip over Dorothy and call my grandmother's name, Margaret, to see if she'd appear to me. I tried this, but she didn't show up, either. Just more bluebells! Oh God, and now I had to share my experience with a perfect stranger!

The woman beside me was all smiles. I could tell that she couldn't wait to tell me what she had experienced, but she asked me to share first.

I told her about the bluebells. Somehow, I felt as though I had failed, but my sharing partner said, "Don't worry, your mother was probably so surprised you were calling her that she didn't know what to do." Then she told me about seeing herself in Egypt as a princess of long, long ago. Her story was so fantastic that my head began to spin. I wondered if she was just a little nuts. It was as though she had been in a movie, watching her lineage line up to greet her. I was speechless and didn't share about the bluebells with anyone else.

My time at Jill's retreat was filled with release, healing, and joy. I spent little time thinking about my mother-lines experience. My effort with my father's lines wasn't any more successful, but I returned home that May knowing I was a new person. Words couldn't do justice to my experience. Many people noticed a difference in me. I felt as though my soul was singing, and I began to feel connected to people. I was no longer living in my ego-psyche somewhere, expecting someone to find the little girl waiting in the hospital for her mother to return. I was beginning to learn how to mother myself, and it would be a year before I would have the opportunity to try again.

The following May, I traveled to Devon, England, once more to experience Jill's week-long retreat at a castle-like place called Hazelwood. Many people had asked what my experience had been like that first year, but it was impossible to explain how singing, chanting, crying, sharing, and loving in a group of almost a hundred people could change your life. But I knew that doing those things could change my life, and I was willing to do them all over again and hopefully go more deeply within myself.

The day arrived when Jill once again guided the group's meditation on our mother's lines. I wasn't as nervous as I had been the first time. I had no expectations. I called my mother's name: Dorothy, Dorothy, Dorothy…and then, surprisingly, before my closed eyes, she appeared. She was younger than when she died, more like forty than sixty, and she was smiling. Apparently, her health was good. She seemed glad to see me. I was astonished to see her. I told her why I had called her—that I wanted to thank her for all she had given me and sacrificed for me; that I wanted us to put all of our suffering, regret, and sorrow in a basket and bury it!

We had begun speaking down by the River Avon on the Hazelwood property. The next thing I knew, she took my hand, and we appeared in front of the house we had lived in, long ago, in Needham, Massachusetts. We brought out a huge cauldron from the inside of the house and put it on the front lawn. We began to drag things out of the house and throw them into the cauldron. I couldn't believe her vitality. The two of us worked until we were exhausted. When the cauldron was filled, we lit the contents—all that had repressed and constricted us in our lives—and watched it burn. She was very happy. So was I. I gave her a large bouquet of flowers as a gift, and that was the end of the vision.

I came out of my trance state feeling happier than I had felt about my mother since I had been a very little girl. Seeing and experiencing her wellness was the biggest and most unexpected gift I could ever have received. I had not realized that anything like this could happen…to me or to anyone else. I had been pretty skeptical about all the stories I heard from others at the retreats. But now this experience of "seeing" my mother increased my awareness that miracles seemingly *could* happen. I couldn't explain the phenomena in my trance state, but I sure knew that something had happened, and I was excited to sense that there was more to life than what I was seeing with my eyes open. There was a whole spiritual world waiting for me to explore.

Over time, I attended seven week-long retreats/ workshops given by Jill Purce, working to free myself from old marks of pain and suffering. Each time, I felt as though pain was lifted from me. The meditations on my mother lines were, by far, the most extraordinary of the extraordinary. The more I experienced the meditation, the further back I went. The following is a synopsis of my mother lines meditation covering the seven intensive retreats I attended:

Each time, I began the meditation by calling my mother's name—Dorothy, Dorothy, Dorothy. After our first meeting, I was able to experience her again and again, in a state of wellness, and was able to move down the line to my grandmother, Margaret.

I called Margaret, Margaret, Margaret…my grandmother appeared as an old woman. She was only forty-seven when she died, but she seemed much older. I tried to speak to her, but she never spoke or smiled. I offered that I would like to help her release what was still holding her in such an apparently sad place, but she never acknowledged me. I gave her the gifts I had for her, which she accepted, and I went on to calling my great-grandmother.

I called Mary Catherine, Mary Catherine, Mary Catherine…Mary Catherine appeared in the blink of an eye. She was an old woman with white hair. She was sitting on a pile of rocks, looking out into Kinvara Bay in Ireland, where she'd been born. She looked straight at me and said she'd been waiting a long time for me to call her. I was amazed, because I had had nothing but an old picture of her that my uncle, Jack—my mother's brother—had given me. He was the family history buff and would search all over for the smallest piece of information about the family, especially from the "old country."

I said, "I'm Maureen, your great-granddaughter."

She told me she knew who I was and that I didn't need to do all that stuff about gifts and putting sufferings in a basket! I burst out laughing. She offered that the biggest suffering in her life had been that five of her six children had emigrated from Ireland, and she had never seen them again. She told me that we had to get going—that she had some place to take me and someone I needed to meet.

"Is it your mother?" I asked her.

We ran as fast as we could, and suddenly, I found myself deep in a forest. My great-grandmother was gone. I could see ahead of me a group of men and women, wearing long coats and capes, gathered around a well. A woman approached and guided me into the center of the circle of people, who seemed extremely happy to see me.

"Come to the well," the woman beckoned me. She dipped a ladle into the water and offered it to me. As I drank the water, I felt as though I had fallen into a magical, green world. When I finished the water, the woman asked me to look into the well. I looked into the well, and what I saw astonished me. I could see my meditation room in my home in Massachusetts. Could they just look into the well and see me any time they wanted? I looked up at the group, and they were beaming. I felt completely filled with joy.

I knew no more names in my mother's line, so I called Mother, Mother, Mother. I found myself in a small town in front of a country store. A woman came out of the store to greet me. I could feel love flowing throughout my body, as she looked at me with her beautiful smile. She appeared to be in her twenties or early thirties and was very, very beautiful, with her long, flowing, red hair.

"It's so wonderful to see you," she told me. She beckoned me to follow her inside the store. She went behind a counter and touched the back wall. The next thing I knew, the wall opened. I was astonished! She motioned me to follow her into what seemed like a cave.

"Where are we?" I asked her. I looked around, and there were shelves everywhere filled with books and scrolls spread out over long tables. "What is this place?" I asked again.

She told me we were in the cave where the Akashic files were kept. "We are the keepers of knowledge," she told me, "We had to hide them. Many wanted to take and destroy them. They don't want us to have this wisdom."

I couldn't believe what I was seeing and hearing. I had heard of the Akashic files only once before. Here was my great-great-great grandmother telling me she was protecting this wisdom from being destroyed. I could hardly believe I was connected to something so amazing.

"Have you met my mother yet?" she asked me.

On my final journey through the mother-lines meditation, everyone along the way, except my grandmother Margaret, encouraged me to travel swiftly through the beautiful places that I had been honored to see and experience. I chanted Mother, Mother, Mother…and then before my closed eyes, she appeared.

I stared and stared. I couldn't figure out who or what I was seeing. There was a face, but no body. The face was absolutely ancient—more ancient than I can describe. This ancient mother smiled at me, and I could feel myself dissolve into love.

"You need to see what you have done," she said to me. "Turn around and look."

I turned around and looked down. I could see the beautiful woman caring for the Akashic files; I could see the people at the well; there was my great-grandmother, my grandmother, my mother, and then there I was. It was me, in that moment, sitting on a cushion in the chapel in Devon, England. I had a shawl around my shoulders, and I was deep into my meditation. Beside everyone in my lineage, there was a lighted streetlamp, the old-fashioned kind you'd see lining the streets of Boston or London.

"You need to see that you have lit the way," she told me. "Look at what you have done! Now," she continued, "you have all the power you need!"

I looked down the line. Everyone seemed at peace. I looked back at her, and she was smiling. My vision of her was swirling around. If I had been filled with any more light or love, I might have exploded. It took me a very, very long time to come back from this meditation. I needed to be in silence for quite a while.

Nothing in my life prepared me for these experiences. I don't know how to explain them, but they happened. It was a journeying with my soul through my maternal lineage, and it gave me a grounding that I had never known. Alysia and Jill had referred to Ancient Mother in their teachings, but I hadn't really visualized her. When I realized it was she who was speaking to me, I was overwhelmed with awe. *Could this be really happening*? I asked myself. And as the question swirled in my head, she was answering with, *Yes, it is me.*

CHAPTER 16
IRISH COUSINS

While attending Jill Purce's workshops in England and beginning to realize the importance of understanding my lineage, I attended a funeral for a relative and ran into my Irish cousins, whom I hadn't seen in a very long time. The oldest of these cousins is Dorothy. She practically ran across the reception room to grab me and give me a big hug and kiss. The force of her embrace almost toppled me, and I'm quite a bit taller than she is. What was even more startling was the way she kept looking at me, as though she was thrilled to see me. "Maureen," she repeated, "how are you, Sweetheart?"

After the reception, I went home and wrote Dorothy a letter telling her how wonderful it had been to see her. But why, I wondered, was she so overjoyed to see me?

She wrote right back. She and her sisters and brothers had grown up with my mother. When I was a baby and my mother was sick, Dorothy's sister, Helen, had taken me in. I could remember Helen very well. She had died many years ago, but I still remembered her warm smile and deep voice.

"Maureen," wrote Dorothy, "we visited you all the time when you were a baby. You were just so beautiful. After Helen had to let you go because her husband was sick with cancer, we tried to see you at the foster-care home, and my brother even visited you at the orphanage. Oh, Maureen, we loved you so much. We kept in touch with your mother the best we could, but after she married your stepfather, she didn't seem to want to have her family calling on her anymore. I think it's because we saw what a hard life she had

had, and we probably brought up these memories.

"But you should know, Maureen, that your mother was a beautiful girl. It was just so hard on her when both her parents died. Our ma wanted to keep your mom and her sister, Mary, but the State told us that we had to have separate bedrooms for them. Can you imagine that, Maureen? There we were with three to four kids to a room, and the state wanted these orphans to have separate bedrooms!

"We were so sad when they couldn't come live with us. Your mother had a real hard time in foster care. She was beautiful, you know, and I think people tried, oh I don't know for sure just what happened to her, but they harassed her, and she'd have nothing to do with that sort of thing. The next you'd hear was that Dottie had been transferred to another home. That went on for both the girls until they graduated from high school.

"She was so young when she married your father. She was eighteen and he was seventeen. Then she had your brother, Howie. He was the most beautiful, blonde baby boy. Your mother kept wondering what was wrong with him. He cried and screamed a lot. You were born thirteen months later—a quiet baby with red curls all over your head. She got no help from your father." (I no longer have the letter, but this is how Dorothy talked and wrote—everything running on with an Irish lilt.)

Dorothy told me she'd love to get together with me anytime I wanted. I was blown away with all this dear woman had shared, and I was amazed that she continued to hold me in such a revered place in her heart. Shortly after our correspondence, I made arrangements to spend some time with Dorothy, and we continued to share our stories.

Soon after I had visited with cousin Dorothy, I told my cousin, Convy, about this new family connection, and she said she wanted to visit the Irish cousins, too! I was so happy to have this new family connection, especially after the work I had done with Jill Purce. For several years, Convy and I had traveled to Lynn, Massachusetts, to visit our cousins. We'd spend the day asking questions about their parents' earlier life in Ireland, and about their own childhoods and life with my mother and Convy's father. In June 2003, we flew to Ireland.

So here we were, Convy and I, traveling to Shannon Airport in Ireland. We rented a car and drove to Galway Bay to meet with our cousins, Louise and Ruthie (Dorothy's younger sisters). They were seventy-five and eighty at the time. We stayed at a bed and breakfast overlooking Galway Bay. Ruthie and Louise made arrangements for us to meet some "real" Irish cousins in Kinvara, just south of Galway, the birthplace of our great-grandparents! The four of us drove to Kinvara in a little, compact car. The countryside was absolutely gorgeous. I had never seen so many different shades of green. I was swept away imagining myself living there or buying a little cottage to visit every year. When I shared this dream with Ruthie and Louise, they laughed and told me that everyone feels that way when they're rediscovering their heritage.

We visited our cousin, John, and his wife at their home just up the road from Kinvara Bay. They were so gracious and told many stories about the "old folks." It seems that my great, great, great, great grandmother's dowry was the sailboat she sailed, on her own, into Kinvara Bay. I couldn't wait to let my son, Michael, know where his passion for sailing came from.

There were stories about gun-running and the "troubles" in Northern Ireland, and it seemed that passions could still be raised by the issue of the British being in Northern Ireland. But cousin John was a poet, an actor, and a singer, and he much preferred to live in peace and sing about the history of Ireland in the pubs at night.

There is a castle in Kinvara. Ruthie and Louise's mother had told them about being a child in Kinvara, with our grandmother. When the tide went out of the bay, they could walk all the way to the castle. All these years later, Convy and I visited the castle in Kinvara and looked back over the bay to the sweet, small town our family had called home. I stood in the tower, gazing over the land and breathing in the air.

"This is where I'm from," I said to myself with great pleasure. A sense of belonging swept over me, as I saw, smelled, and tasted the salt air. I have always been drawn to the ocean. I thought it was because I had been born in Gloucester, Massachusetts, a fishing town on the Atlantic Ocean. But standing by the bay in Kinvara gave me a sense of my lineage—my roots that ran all the way to Ireland. *I felt like I was home.*

Convy and I spent a day on our own, wandering the streets in Kinvara. We looked into all the small shops and stopped to have lunch. Later, we walked down the street where our great-grandmother had lived and tried to figure out just where her home had stood. At the end of the street was the bay with a stone wall around its edges. We each posed for a picture, sitting on that wall of stones. I thought of my great grandmother, as I had seen her in my visions in Devon. I closed my eyes and told her that I had come back to see the place where she had waited for me to call her name.

Before we left Kinvara, Convy needed to mail some postcards. As I browsed through the quaint post office, I noticed a book about Kinvara, which included old photographs of the town and its people. Back at the inn that evening, I looked through the book, enjoying the pictures. There, before my eyes, was a picture of several men standing on the street where our great grandmother had lived. These men, according to the caption, were repairing sails for the boats of fishermen in town. Their names were listed, and three of the men were our great-uncles!

Our trip was only four days long, but filled with the essence of heritage. I felt so connected to my Irish lineage. As a small child and even into early adulthood, I didn't feel great about being Irish. It's one of the reasons I could give up the name Maureen so easily. My early experiences—of my mother's troubled life and my own low self-esteem—created a stigma for me: a sense of inferiority as a Boston Irish Catholic girl whose father had abandoned her. I felt rejected by my Catholic friends and relatives, who openly ridiculed me because my mother had divorced. In fourth grade, a nun shrieked in front of the entire class that my mother was going to hell because she was divorced. She continued with, "Who knows what's going to happen to Maureen?" This kind of ignorance colored my view of being Irish.

What a blessing it was to find such strong and vital cousins who gave me hope of living past the age of sixty and into my nineties! Through this experience, I was able to issue a hearty thank you to the women who had come before me, for waiting so patiently for me to call them forth, in order that I might know what greatness I came from.

CHAPTER 17
A TIME TO MEET

Two months after Jill Purce's Healing Voice workshop, at which I heard Ancient Mother tell me that I had all the power I needed, I was watching a movie on television while ironing Larry's golf shirts.

I actually don't mind ironing; it softens my mind. It was a rainy, muggy July day, and watching a Lifetime movie about a distressed woman who finally got out of a bad relationship and triumphed over life's adversities helped pass the time.

The telephone rang.

"Hello," I said.

"Hi Kris, it's Kyra!"

It had been almost ten months since our first conversation, and I hadn't heard from her since. I was completely taken by surprise. In fact, I was shocked! I had to sit down and drink some water.

"You do remember who this is, don't you?" she said.

"Of course I do," I replied.

"Well," she said, "I think it's time that we make a date to meet each other."

"That would be great," I replied, wondering in the back of my mind why it had taken her this long to call me back,

"How about next week?"

She agreed, and we chose a meeting place.

I felt excited and afraid at the same time. Many people have asked me over the years how I felt getting ready for the day I would meet Kyra. The feelings were so enormous and all encompassing that I felt like my body was trying to catch up with my mind—which was spinning. At the same time, my heart was about to explode.

I was like a nervous cat when the day arrived. We had arranged to meet in front of St. Mary's church on the main road in Longmeadow, Massachusetts. It was a beautiful, summer day with a nice breeze. I got there early. There weren't any people around. I sat in my car thinking: *This is unbelievable.* My throat felt dry, and I wondered how I would survive this meeting. I realized I was really scared. *What would she think of me? Would she like me?* I felt like I was jumping into the abyss.

I recognized her car. She had described it for me. It was a large SUV. As she pulled into the parking lot, I could hardly breathe. I watched her get out of her car and open the back door to get her little boy from his car seat.

She looked at me with a smile, and I thought, *She doesn't look like me at all! I am very fair skinned with blue eyes, and she has dark brown hair with brown eyes.*

Her first words were, "Well, we don't look anything alike!"

We hugged, and she introduced me to two-year-old Phillip. He was just waking up from his nap in the car and needed to hold onto his mother tightly. He had a sweet smile on a pie-shaped face, big brown eyes, and sandy colored hair. He was beautiful. I couldn't stop staring at both of them. This was really happening! I could hardly speak. After all the years of wondering and imagining, here they were right before me. I was awestruck.

We went to a nearby park so he could run and play on the swings. Here I was with the woman who was my daughter, and yet I didn't know her at all. She didn't know me, either.

She asked a lot of questions about me and my family, and about her birth father, which I answered. She seemed satisfied.

I had brought a camera with me. I thought that if I never saw them again, at least I'd have a picture of us to show my family. So before we left the park to go to lunch, I asked a passerby to take our picture.

At lunch, we talked about our likes and dislikes regarding food and weather and trivial things like that. As I sat across from her, I began to see that she was actually a darker version of me. She had many of my facial characteristics. As I was thinking this, she piped in with, "I think Phillip looks a lot like you!" I guess we were both trying to find some physical connection to each other. I had brought her a gift: a blue stone in the shape of a heart on a silver chain. She seemed very touched when I gave it to her.

I asked if we could see each other again.

She was hesitant. "Maybe," she said. "My boyfriend didn't want me to contact you. He said that you had abandoned me as a baby, so why would I want to know you now?" Wow, she didn't mince words, and her words hurt. I don't know what I expected…I guess I really thought she would say: *Absolutely, I want to see you again, because I've waited most of my life to meet my birth mother, and you seem amazing. I really want to get to know you and be a part of your family.* That's what I wanted to hear. What she actually said, however, cut to the bone, and I had no voice to reply to her. Maybe I thought I deserved it.

There wasn't much I could think of to say in response, except that I hoped that now that we had met, she might consider meeting the rest of the family. She told me she really wanted to meet Joan and Michael, because she had never known any blood relatives in her life. That sounded hopeful to me.

Then it was time for them to leave. While Kyra put Phillip into his car seat, we told each other we'd meet again soon. We hugged goodbye, and then she got into her car and drove off.

I watched the car disappear down the road. *People have no idea what other people are doing in parking lots*, I thought. My whole life had just been altered, and to the casual observer, we merely looked like women saying goodbye to each other after lunch.

I walked straight to the sixty-minute photo section in the drugstore and waited for the film to develop. I wanted to have something in my hands when I got home to prove that the day had actually happened.

I showed the pictures to Larry right away. He was very excited for me and had many questions about our visit. I told him everything we had talked about, and how it had felt to finally be with Kyra and Phillip.

I had told Kyra that a meeting with Joan and Michael could take place as soon as the following week, because Joan—who lived in Minnesota and returned infrequently—would be visiting.

But when the evening of the meeting approached, Kyra called to say that she wasn't coming. She had a very bad headache. I was disappointed for all the obvious reasons: I doubted that a headache was the real reason she wouldn't be coming, but more importantly, I knew it would be a long time before we could arrange for another meeting.

Kyra had given me her address and telephone number. She was living with her boyfriend, not Phillip's father. She had sole custody of Phillip. Phillip's birth father had no contact with him. This had been court-ordered because of his drug use. Phillip considered this boyfriend to be his daddy. Since Kyra had made it very clear to me that her boyfriend didn't want her to see me, I wasn't surprised at not hearing from her again after the initial calls. However, when I knew that Joan would be in town again two months later, I called Kyra and left a message to tell her that the meeting could still be arranged. I was delighted when she called to say she would meet us at a restaurant in Connecticut the following week.

Larry arranged for us to have a very private table in an alcove of the restaurant. I was so nervous and excited. A few minutes after we arrived, Kyra entered and was shown to our seat. She and Joan looked at each other and hugged. It was amazing to see them together. I had never actually imagined them embracing, and witnessing it made my heart feel like exploding with happiness. Several minutes later, Michael came in, and Kyra just jumped into his arms. I was surprised to witness so much emotion from Michael and Joan, because they had seemed pretty nervous about the meeting. This was a huge event for them, and they were obviously happy to meet and hug their new, older sister.

It could not have been a sweeter evening. Although positively surreal, those moments were pure joy for me. All I could do was to sit back and look at all three of my children, together for the first time. I couldn't stop smiling. Larry was a prince as he kept the conversation going whenever we fell silent. He kept us laughing and feeling safe as we began this new relationship. And, of course, I had my camera ready. I finally had a picture of all three of them: Michael, Joan, and Kyra.

When Joan later saw the picture, she said, "Mom, it looks like I'm the daughter you found, because Michael and Kyra look so much alike." Another picture of the five of us still brings me to tears whenever I look at it. My face was illuminated with love.

I didn't have to do any work at that first dinner meeting. The three young people kept talking and laughing, trying to fit the puzzle pieces together. "Are you really my mom's daughter?" "Are you really my sister?" "Do I really have siblings I'm related to by blood?"

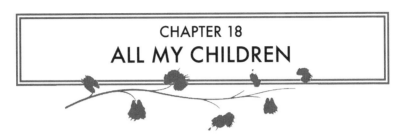

CHAPTER 18
ALL MY CHILDREN

The holiday season was approaching, and I dared to ask Kyra to come for Christmas dinner. To my surprise, she agreed to come. The weeks approaching Christmas were filled with anxiety and foreboding. By the time Christmas day arrived, I could hardly put two sentences together. I couldn't figure out why I wasn't on top of the world, knowing that all of my children would be together on Christmas day.

Thank goodness that I have such a wonderful family. Alysia was also helpful to me during this time. She reminded me that I probably still had many unresolved emotions about the birth of Kyra. I had dreaded Christmas Day those many years ago, because I would have to give Kyra up for adoption soon after. Despite all my work in the healing workshops, a part of me was still living in that anxiety-filled place where I felt helpless and vulnerable without power to change my life. At least it was comforting to understand my inner dynamics.

Kyra and Phillip arrived Christmas afternoon, and we exchanged gifts. It was so amazing to have them in our home—and a little strange, too. Here was the missing daughter with her son preparing to sit at our holiday table. It was like something out of a *Hallmark Hall of Fame* movie, only it was really happening. We shared our traditional turkey dinner—everyone except Joan, a vegetarian who ate tofu-turkey. Then we dove into the many pies we had for dessert.

Kyra told us stories of her life. The family I had surrendered her to was not so perfect after all. Kyra had a sister, five years older who was her parents' birth-child. I hadn't been told that when I agreed to the adoption. I thought they had adopted their first child, and Kyra would be their second.

This matters because, when Kyra was five years old, the older sister told her that she had been adopted and that only she, the birth-daughter, was the real child! This had been very traumatic for Kyra. Kyra told us that from that day on she wondered, "Where is my mother?"

Eventually she also had an adopted brother, five years her junior. She felt closer to him simply because they shared a similar birth history.

Kyra admitted to us that despite a very affluent childhood that included private schools, she had always been rambunctious and rebellious. Her parents divorced when she was ten years old, and that threw the family into chaos. Wars broke out among all the family members.

Her father, an apparent emotional bully, informed the children that if they decided to live with their mother instead of with him, he would basically disown them. Kyra was the only child to stay with her mother. This set up a family dynamic that continued to that day.

Eventually, both parents remarried, and Kyra traveled back and forth between the families for many years. She told us her father still derided her whenever he got the chance.

This was a lot to share at Christmas dinner. I felt deeply disappointed that Kyra's parents didn't seem to be the "perfect" parents to whom I thought I had given her.

It seems that Kyra's stepmother had a positive influence on her regarding education—encouraging her to become a nurse so that she could earn a livable income. When we first met, Kyra was a Licensed Practical Nurse (LPN) at an adult psychiatric hospital. It astonished me that she was working in a place that could have housed my brother, Howard—Kyra's uncle.

She shared stories about the difficult relationship she had always had with her older sister. It seemed there were many months and years of silence between them. Arguing was the way her family communicated. She still hadn't told anyone in her family that she was in contact with us. I wondered if she ever would feel safe enough to tell them.

The week following Christmas, Larry and I set off for a Florida vacation for six weeks. It felt good to be going away. The time leading up to Christmas and the actual event took a lot out of me. I felt emotionally spent. I had just experienced one of the most amazing days of my life: all my family together for Christmas. But it drained me—because of all the ambiguities about my relationship with Kyra.

It had been momentous leading up to Christmas, and now it felt anticlimactic, because Kyra couldn't say if she wanted a relationship with me or with her sister and brother. Larry had recently retired from his real estate company, so we could finally take a long-awaited, extended vacation. Kyra had asked that I call her when we got to Florida to let her know we had arrived safely. We were driving, so there was no set time when we would arrive.

I was on a really big learning curve when it came to handling my relationship with Kyra. I was still nervous to be with her and talk to her on the telephone. Therefore, when I got to Florida, calling Kyra was not the first thing I did. Instead, I went food shopping and got used to my surroundings. The first night there, Larry and I actually went out to dinner and toasted our good lives.

The next day, Joan called to say that Kyra had emailed her and was worried about us. "Maybe you should call her, Mom," she said.

When I called Kyra, she started yelling at me because I hadn't called her immediately, and she had been very worried. Oh boy! I guess I was a little too laid back for her. I apologized and told her I was very touched that it mattered so much to her that I was safe. The upside of this was that she cared so much and probably didn't want to lose me again. The downside was that I don't do well when people yell at me. I found her reaction to be unnerving.

One evening in Florida, we came home after a wonderful birthday dinner celebrating my special day. On the answering machine was a beautiful message from Kyra wishing me the happiest of birthdays.

Never in my life had I imagined receiving a message like that from my daughter, whom I hadn't known for thirty-three years. It was wonderful.

I called to thank her for the gift of her loving message and got her machine. I called a few days later and got her machine. She didn't call back. I tried once more, but I began to feel silly talking to a machine.

Several months later, near Phillip's birthday, I called Kyra again. She picked up the phone. She told me she was preparing for Phillip's birthday party and expected many friends to come and celebrate later in the day. I told her I had missed her and wondered why she hadn't returned any of my calls. With that, she shouted, "I don't need this kind of aggravation in my life. This is all too much for me, and I don't want to talk to you!" Then she hung up on me.

I sat there in shock and burst into tears. "Could this be the end after all we've been through?" I wondered. It had taken courage to call Kyra, and it was devastating to hear her speak to me with so much anger. I decided to leave Kyra to her feelings and not expect her to understand mine. It was hard, but I had to step back.

A lot was going on in Kyra's life when she was reuniting with me. She still wasn't able to tell her family about meeting us. She was living with a man who was physically abusive. He didn't support her contacting me. She admitted that they had used drugs recreationally and alcohol to excess, and she didn't know if she could stay with him any longer. She wasn't seeing anyone who could counsel her.

I was appalled that she was living with such a violent man, and I had encouraged her to leave him. But I was walking a thin line. I had no authority in her life. She hadn't asked for my advice. Responding like a mother, when she already had a mother, was confusing and not helpful.

I felt confused, too. *Who was I really to her? Who was she really to me? What was my role in Kyra's life? Did I have a role in Kyra's life? Did she even want me in her life.*

I heard from Kyra nine months later. She was in a good mood and sounded happy. She spoke as though we had never had any harsh words between us.

She whispered into the phone, "Kris, he's a lot better now. He's been so good to me lately, and he even said it's okay that I contact you again!"

Happy as I was to hear from her, my heart sank with the realization that she was in such an unhealthy, codependent relationship. If that telephone call had come from Joan or Michael, I would have been all over it like a mother bear protecting her cubs. But I had no power to influence Kyra's behavior, and I felt helpless to do anything.

It would be a very long time before I heard from Kyra again.

CHAPTER 19
SURPRISE!

Several times over the years, I was contacted by the Massachusetts Department of Mental Health and asked if I had any information regarding my father's Social Security number. If I could supply that number, then my brother would be allocated more funds. The people who called always sounded surprised that I had absolutely no idea of the whereabouts of my father, let alone his Social Security number.

A young man new to the system had been assigned to my brother's case. When he called and asked me for the same information, I answered, again, that I had no idea where my father was, much less his Social Security number. He was very personable, and we talked for a while about my brother. He asked me if it would be okay if he did some research to locate my father. I said I was fine with that, and off he went to the Internet to begin his search.

A week or so later, he called to tell me he had come across my father's name on a list of deceased people in California. He doubted that it was actually my father, though, because the birth date didn't match other records. My father's date of birth on his marriage license wasn't the same as the one on the list of deceased he had come upon. When we compared the dates, however, I was able to confirm that the date on the list of deceased was correct for Lewis Howard Publicover—the date on the marriage certificate was incorrect. We both got very excited to think that we had made the right connections. He told me he would request a copy of the death certificate immediately, and get back to me as soon as possible.

I put down the telephone and stared off into space. The shock of hearing that my father was dead was setting in. I hardly knew how to feel. I think I mostly felt disappointed that I would never meet him. After all these years, I had found my father, and he was dead. How strange never to have known him.

A couple of weeks later, I heard from the mental health worker. He had a copy of Lewis Howard Publicover's death certificate, and would send a copy to me right away. The death certificate said that Lewis had died in 1988 at the age of sixty from pulmonary heart disease. He had been a short-order cook and had left a wife named Barbara. *He left a wife named Barbara!* The young man said he was going to contact Barbara Publicover to request my father's Social Security number, and he agreed to ask if she would be willing to speak to me. I couldn't believe it. Maybe I could ask her about my father.

He called me back several days later and said that Barbara was willing to talk to me. He gave me her telephone number.

Larry wanted me to make a list of questions a mile long to ask Barbara, but I could hardly speak when I finally dialed her telephone number.

A woman with a harsh-sounding voice answered the phone—like someone who had smoked a lot.

"Hello," I said. "This is Maureen Publicover Landry. I don't know if you ever knew about me, but it seems your late husband was my father. "

"Yes, I knew about you!" she told me.

"Okay," I said. "I just want to find out a few things about my father since I never knew him."

"Well, whaddaya wanna know?" she asked me.

Oh God, I wasn't good at this. I have a number of friends who could have done a great interrogation of this woman, but I was feeling overwhelmed.

She broke the silence by telling me that Lewis had been a good husband and a great father.

"Oh," I said, "you have children."

"Yes," she replied. "We had three children: Laurie's in Las Vegas; Craig's in Arizona; and Christine's in California."

My head was spinning. I had three more siblings! "Do you think you could send me some pictures of my father?" I asked her.

"They're all packed away," she told me, "But maybe I could dig some out for you."

I thanked her very much, and she said to call again if I wanted to talk some more.

"What did she say?" Larry wanted to know.

"I have two more sisters and a brother," I replied. He couldn't believe I didn't get their addresses or telephone numbers. But I just couldn't get the words out. Barbara didn't seem like she wanted me to get in touch with her children. It was a feeling I got from the sound of her voice.

I needed to sit with this new information. My heart was pounding. We called Joan and Michael and said, "Guess what?"

"Not another sister," Michael laughingly replied.

"Not for you, but for me. Two, actually, and a brother."

Michael took my new sibling's names and searched on the Internet for their addresses and telephone numbers.

He found them. I couldn't call any of them for many, many months. I would look at their numbers and practice what I would say, and then feel exhausted and put the list away. This went on for six months before I finally got up the nerve to call my brother, Craig.

CHAPTER 20
MEETING IN LAS VEGAS

I dialed Craig's number, and a woman answered. I asked to speak to Craig, and she asked with great authority, "Who wants to know?"

With that, I began to laugh and said, "Well, there is no easy way to say this, but my name is Maureen Landry, and I'm Craig's older sister."

"Oh, my God, it's *you!*" she screamed into the phone. "We were just talking about you, Maureen. Craig's mother visited us last week and just told us about you."

I was calling just a week after Barbara told her children about me. It was as though I couldn't call them until she had told them.

The woman kept screaming happily, telling me she'd run and get Craig. "Craig, Craig, it's your sister, Maureen, on the phone for you!" I could hear her say.

A man with the softest and most gentle voice came to the receiver. "Hello, Maureen, I'm Craig, your brother." It was an amazing moment for both of us. Every word spoken was magic to me. Craig said, "I'm so sorry my mother didn't tell us about you sooner. We think she was keeping the secret our dad wanted her to keep. We were so upset she didn't tell us after he died."

What do you say, when you're in your fifties, to a brother you are meeting for the first time? We kept asking questions: "When's your birthday? Do you have children?" We didn't want to hang up, but finally, reluctantly, we said goodbye, promising to keep in touch. I got off the phone with tears in my eyes and my heart swollen with emotion.

It was two weeks before I was ready to call Laurie in Las Vegas. I waited until evening, keeping in mind she worked full-time and lived in a different time zone. As I walked to the telephone to call her, it rang.

It was Laurie! Craig had given her my number. She had a bright, happy voice. She said, "Maureen, it's your sister."

There I was again, feeling myself explode with emotion. She was so sweet, telling me how happy she was to find out she had an older sister. Her daughter, Adrianna, was thrilled she was to have a new aunt! We also promised to stay in touch with each other.

It wasn't twenty-four hours later when the telephone rang and a loud, hoarse, happy voice boomed, "Hey, Maureen, this is your sister, Christine!"

What a wonderful character she was. "Maureen," she told me, "I always knew my father had his secrets, and I suspected he may have had other children. His favorite Hollywood actress was Maureen O'Hara. When he would say her name, I knew someone named Maureen had meant something very special to him." She was blowing my mind! I hardly knew what to do with what she was telling me. "I want to meet you, Maureen," she said to me.

I promised to figure out a way for all of us to get together.

We made plans to meet in Las Vegas in July 2001. I was amazed at what was happening to me. Larry and I made reservations at the Mirage Hotel. Craig and his wife, Diane, drove up from Arizona; Christine and her boyfriend, Richard, drove in from Oakland, California; and Laurie, of course, was already there.

Our plan was to meet for brunch at one of the restaurants in the hotel. Larry spoke to the manager of the restaurant and reserved a large, round table in a private area, clueing her in as to what was about to happen. Larry's orders to me were to get up early and eat breakfast, because he knew I wouldn't be able to eat a thing once I met the rest of my family.

As the moment we were to meet each other for the first time approached, I stood at the restaurant's entrance, leaning on a decorative column on the pathway to the casinos. Hordes of people streamed from all directions. I scanned every group, wondering, "Are you my family?"

Larry put his hand on my shoulder and remarked, "Honey, I think you can eliminate the Asian and African-American families walking by."

I burst out laughing.

Then I heard a voice. "There she is; it's Maureen!" A beautiful young girl was leading an excited group of people who called out my name.

I looked at them, and they looked at me. I couldn't move. Larry put his arm around me and guided me into the restaurant, leading the band of followers to our table.

We stared at each other.

Craig looked at me and smiled. "Hello, Maureen." Then he hugged me.

Laurie sat next to me and grabbed my arm. "Oh, my God, you're my sister. I'm so happy to finally be meeting you." She literally checked out my every feature and compared what similarities we had.

"You look just like Craig!" Christine exclaimed. "And you and I have the same nose!"

Little Adrianna never took the smile off of her face.

Larry was right. I couldn't eat a thing. It was so wonderful and very overwhelming. Craig had brought a photo album and showed me pictures of them as children with their parents. They kept referring to their mom and dad. It was strange to hear the word *dad*. I had never gotten to call anyone *Dad*, and here they were talking about their dad and mine.

As brunch was coming to an end, Craig asked us if we had any plans that evening. We didn't, so we agreed to meet at Laurie's for a cookout. Craig offered to pick us up. The plan sounded great. My head was about to fall off. Just a couple of hours with my new siblings, and I needed a nap. I could feel my skin breaking out from the stress, but I was very happy. In my wildest imagination, I had never thought I would experience a day like this. Words are insufficient to express the delight in my heart. With my brother, Howie, sent away and my sister, Beverly, being so much younger than me, I felt lonely as a child. This was like out of a storybook.

CHAPTER 21
FAMILY STORIES

Craig and Diane picked us up in front of the hotel, and Diane insisted that I sit up front with my brother. It was very sweet to sit beside *my brother* on the way to *my sister's* house.

Adrianna bounded out the door, and Laurie met us with her bright and wonderful smile. Christine and Richard were there to greet us, too. It was time to take pictures. They wanted the photos as much as I did! When I look at those pictures today, they bring me smiles and deep happiness. Because my brother, Howie, was taken from my home when I was so young, I grew up my first ten years as an only child. Now, here we stood, four of our father's five children, smiling with joy.

After a meal of salad, hamburgers, and Diet Dr. Pepper, Craig, Laurie, Christine, and I sat around Laurie's round dining-room table. In that moment, I realized I actually didn't have much to tell them. I shared about my mother and Howie and what little I knew about our father's family. They were fascinated to hear about Howie, and wanted to know everything I could tell them.

Very soon, my brother and two sisters began to talk about their lives. When I had spoken to their mother, Barbara, I had gotten the impression that she and our father had been married for more than thirty years. That wasn't the case. I learned that Barbara and our father were married for less than ten years. After divorcing our father, she married a couple more times, and divorced, before getting back with him. Barbara was an alcoholic—a very bad alcoholic.

Our father, Lewis, was a tough character as well. He drank hard, gambled hard, and things had better go his way, or else! After Barbara and Lewis separated, Lewis broke a sliding glass door to enter their home and kidnap the children. Barbara never reported it to the police—she was a very dysfunctional alcoholic—so my father never felt in jeopardy of losing them. They didn't see their mother again for many, many years. "Maybe he just couldn't give up his kids again," Christine suggested.

The three children moved from town to town with their father, who went from racetrack to racetrack around the country. For an entire year, they lived in one room in a motel. They told stories of their favorite nanny, who was a bartender friend of their father. He cooked them dinner and sometimes read them bedtime stories. At times, they had to get out of town quickly because of gambling debts, leaving behind the few possessions they owned. They had fond memories of time spent in Florida at a trailer camp, but the best times were with their mother's parents in California.

Craig was very quiet. He said he didn't like to dwell on his childhood. As a boy, he would read the Bible with a little light underneath his blankets. That was the only comfort he had as a child. Laurie, on the other hand, put as much sunshine into her stories as she could. Christine recalled that one day her father hauled off and punched her in the face. That was when she decided to move out on her own.

Every fantasy I ever had about my father evaporated. As lonely and isolated as my childhood had seemed to me, I realized I had dodged a big, fat bullet. I could not have stood the violence or even the threat of violence. My mother's emotional illness seemed mild compared to the life that these three had endured with our father. Yet, despite how difficult their young lives had been, none of them wanted to speak ill of their parents. They were just telling me the facts.

After many years of no contact with their mother, they secretly arranged to reunite with her. They met her near the Ferris wheel at the Santa Monica pier. They had decided it was time to speak to her themselves. It was hard for them, and for Barbara too, but they needed to be close again. When they eventually told their father what they'd done, he didn't seem to mind. In fact, Laurie moved in with her mother to finish high school, and he didn't resist it.

As the years went on, their father was living in a men's rooming-house, and Barbara was alone, three times divorced. They actually fixed their parents up on a date, which resulted in their marrying again. The drinking had stopped, and in their older years, their behavior had modified so much that at the sight of each other, they didn't erupt into anger. They actually became friends again.

In 1988, Barbara and Lewis decided to take a trip to Las Vegas. They hadn't been away in years. On the morning of the scheduled trip, Barbara went to see if her husband was up for breakfast. Instead, she found him in bed, dead. I said I thought it was remarkable that the four of us were having our first get-away together in Las Vegas. They nodded in agreement.

Our good-byes were bittersweet, because we didn't know when we would see each other again. After many kisses and hugs, Craig and Diane dropped us off at our hotel.

Sometimes, a moment, an experience, is so big that it's hard to put it into words. This was one of those events. My perception of my life had just shifted. For days, I found myself daydreaming through the images of all that had happened—finding what had been missing from my life.

I hadn't known the emotional impact of living with the absence of so many people related to me: my father, my developmentally challenged brother, my daughter, my grandson, two sisters, and a brother. Including my sister Beverly from my mother's second marriage, I am one of six siblings. While I had felt like an orphan much of my life, I discovered that I was part of a large family.

Flying home from Las Vegas, I stared into the clouds and thought about all of the missing people I had found. I had never realized how deep and wide the empty space inside of me had been. Only after claiming what was mine did I begin to realize the toll of so much disconnection. My connection to the universe had been that of disconnection. Now I could live in a new space, in a relationship with what was once missing and now found.

CHAPTER 22
AN EXTRAORDINARY OPPORTUNITY

On September 10, 2001, the Landry family gathered together to attend an evening Mass honoring the memory of Larry's dad, Norman. He had passed away one year before at the age of ninety-two. Larry's sister, Celine, and her husband, Bob, spent the night at our home, planning to return to their home on Cape Cod the following day.

As I was making breakfast the next morning, I watched—as did many millions of others around the world—the horrific scenes of the attack on the World Trade Center in New York City. I quite literally wondered if the end of the world was at hand. I called Joan, who was then living in Portland, Oregon, a three-hour-earlier time zone, and told her to get out of bed and turn on her television. For days, it seemed, I watched CNN for ten-hour stretches. Surely, the world had changed overnight.

It was shortly after the catastrophic events of 9/11 that Kyra called and left a long message on my answering machine. She wanted me to call her as soon as possible. I hardly knew what to expect. I was able to reach her immediately.

"I'm calling you, Kris," she began in her voicemail message, "because after the events of 9/11, I know that life is too short. But what has really compelled me to call you is that my mother died last week of cancer, and I'm devastated. I'm not sure why I'm really saying all of this to you, but I want you to know that I want a relationship with you and your family. I want to tell you that I love you very much. I'm no longer with my boyfriend. I finally made the decision to leave him after he struck Phillip. My father has helped me to relocate. I want you to know that I'm starting my life over with a clean slate, and I want you to be part of it!"

I was astonished and amazed by Kyra's words. Maybe she was finally ready for what she was proposing. I was skeptical, but I wanted us to try again. We made arrangements to meet at her new apartment, also in Connecticut, several days later. Larry and I would take Kyra and Phillip out to dinner.

It took us several hours to get to her new address. It had been almost two years since I had last seen her, and I was nervous and excited to be with her again. I spent the time in the car going over our previous conversations and experiences. *She was inviting me into her world for the third time.* I was aware that she seemed to have an issue sustaining relationships. When they didn't feel good to her, she bolted and disappeared.

She opened the apartment door, looking beautiful and petite. Phillip, the toddler I had known, was now a little boy who wanted to show us everything in his bedroom. It was filled with books and toys. Clearly, Kyra loved her son. He was immaculate and beautifully dressed. He wanted to be part of everything that was going on. He wanted to play, but he wanted to listen to our conversations too. He seemed accustomed to being part of an adult world.

We found a wonderful Italian restaurant. Phillip couldn't get enough of Larry, and Larry was like the Pied Piper with Phillip. We ordered cocktails before dinner. Phillip occupied himself with several dinosaurs from his collection. He knew all of their names. Kyra seemed relaxed after her cocktail and ordered another one, along with Larry. I sipped my wine, once again experiencing how surreal it was to be with her again.

She wanted to know how Larry and I had gotten together. We regaled her with stories about the Outside In and the Prince Spaghetti Minstrels, and told her how we had married five months after we'd met.

"Let me get this straight," she exclaimed, leaning closer to my face, "you mean to tell me you gave me away one year, and the next year you married him? Why couldn't you have done it the other way around?"

What could I say in response to that question? I was astonished that she was so bold. Obviously, on some level, she was showing her approval of Larry, and maybe subconsciously she was thinking that he could have been her father. There was no answer for her. Dinner came to a close, and we walked back to the parking lot. I can still see Phillip happily sitting atop Larry's shoulders as we searched for our car.

Kyra and I spoke on the telephone, on and off, for several weeks, keeping each other abreast of what was going on in our lives. We made plans for them to come to our home for Sunday dinner. Larry is a wonderful cook, and he promised to prepare an Italian feast. The week before our dinner engagement, Kyra said that she had something very important she wanted to speak to me about. She would talk to me in private when she and Phillip came to dinner. I couldn't imagine what it was about. I talked with Larry, and we mulled over possibilities. I thought she might want to ask me to be in some kind of guardianship position for Phillip, in case something happened to her, because I was his grandmother, the closest blood relative he seemed destined to know.

The two of them arrived happy and hungry. They thought Larry was the best cook ever. As we were clearing the dishes, Kyra looked at me and said, "You know, you really made out getting him," pointing to Larry.

I told her that I knew I was a very fortunate woman.

"Do you have any idea," she went on, "how hard it is to be a single mother?"

I said I could only imagine how difficult it was to work all day and care for a young child alone.

She looked around my kitchen, which was beautiful and large, and said, "You really got lucky getting a guy like him."

Again, I affirmed that I knew I was blessed.

"You know," she said, "my father helped me move to my new area, because he said that's where I'd find a million dollar penis!"

I was speechless. I think she thought I had found one. "Let's go for a walk," I stammered.

She thought that was a good idea, because she could have a cigarette. We walked along the streets in my neighborhood. It seemed so natural.

"Kyra, we have an extraordinary opportunity before us," I said. "After all these years, we've finally met, and I think we have a chance of building a relationship. We can take it slowly, without pressure. I want you to know how much I would like us to have, at the very least, a friendship."

She nodded in agreement. Then, little Phillip jumped out of the woods and ran after us. "Hey," he said, "how come you went on a walk without me?"

CHAPTER 23
RETURN TO SENDER

Back at the house, Kyra began gathering their things together for the trip home. "Kris," she said, "I need to talk to you about that matter I mentioned."

"Of course," I nodded and ushered us into a private area.

She began by saying that she would be receiving money from her mother's estate within the next six weeks, but until that time, she had no money to pay her bills. She had just started a new job and hadn't been paid yet. She opened a small jewelry box that held a diamond brooch. "Kris, I need twenty-five hundred dollars. I'd be willing to leave this pin that belonged to my grandmother with you, until I could repay this loan." I must have looked surprised. "I can't go to my father for any more money!" she exclaimed.

I told her I needed to speak to Larry.

I went into the other room and motioned to Larry to come over to me. I shared what Kyra had just said.

He looked concerned. "I'll see if we can cover it," he told me. He came back with a check for twenty-five hundred dollars made out to Kyra. "Tell her not to leave the diamond pin," he said.

I gave the check to her. She was thrilled and threw her arms around me, thanking me over and over again. The two of them got into their car, drove out of the driveway, and turned the corner out of my sight. I wondered when I would ever see them again.

Admittedly, I was disappointed that what Kyra wanted from us was money. It's my experience that money complicates relationships, especially ones like ours, which we were still trying to get off the ground. Larry was disappointed at this new turn of events, too. He felt that it put unnecessary pressure on all of us.

Kyra called the following week, thanking us for a wonderful and delicious dinner. She expressed how happy she had felt just being with us and how peaceful our home had seemed to her.

We had spoken about the possibility of Kyra and Phillip coming for Thanksgiving dinner. I was excited, because it would be the first time I could share them with more members of our family. She said she very much wanted to come, but felt that since she still hadn't told her family about reuniting with me, it might be difficult.

On the morning of Thanksgiving, I called Kyra, and she answered with, "Oh, we were just going to call you. You know I'd rather spend the day with you and Larry, but I just can't." She couldn't get out of spending the holiday with her father and stepmother's family.

We were both disappointed, but I told her I understood, and we assured each other that we loved one another and would talk very soon. I was left with a heart brimming with hope and love.

The day after Thanksgiving, I called Kyra and got her answering machine. I left a message welcoming her home, hoping that her long ride in traffic had gone well. I didn't hear from her. I let a week go by and tried again. She didn't pick up or call back. I was dumbfounded! What had happened this time? Could spending the day with her father have been so confusing and stressful for her that balancing her family relationship with our secret relationship proved overwhelming? I knew from Kyra's stories that her relationship with her father was emotionally packed. On the one hand, he was generous with his financial support, but on the other, he was dictatorial about how she was to live her life. She had told us she felt as though she was a "screw-up" in his eyes. Maybe dinner on Thanksgiving Day with her father made her feel guilty about not having told him about me. These were the questions that raced across my mind. *How could she be so seemingly sincere about her love and desire to become a part of our family, and then disappear again?*

As disappointed as I was, I also felt sad for her. She seemed to take one step forward and two steps backward when it came to our getting closer.

Christmas was coming. It was always an emotionally loaded time for me. Nonetheless, I loved shopping for Kyra and Philip. Being able to send her a card on her birthday meant everything to me. I sent the packages off early, hoping to elicit a response. The day before Christmas, the packages were returned to sender. I burst into tears. I had a house full of company and meals to plan and prepare. I was so happy that Joan and Michael were coming home for Christmas. I couldn't let this mar my holidays. I put the packages in the front hall closet and didn't touch them again.

CHAPTER 24
HOW COME YOU GAVE
MY MOTHER AWAY?

Months passed. I asked Larry what he thought about Kyra's disappearance. He wondered if she had become embarrassed about borrowing money from us and not paying back the loan. I decided to write a letter with the hope that it would be forwarded to her new address, although the Christmas packages had not.

I wrote to her and told her how sad I was not to be hearing from her again, and that I wanted to bring up the awkward situation of money. I told her we didn't want the money to stand in the way of our speaking to each other. If she was embarrassed, I said, she should know we would try to understand whatever circumstances had forced her to stop communicating with us. I included a card for Phillip's birthday with a small remembrance inside and sent it off. *At least*, I thought, *I'm doing something.* But still, we didn't hear from her. The good news, however, was that the mail was not returned to sender. Life went on. Birthdays and holidays came and went. We heard nothing from Kyra.

Larry and I began spending more and more time in Florida. He had taken me to Florida kicking and screaming, but now he couldn't get me to leave. I loved the weather, and I felt physically well all the time. The cold of the north and the change of seasons had played havoc with my allergies for many years. The respite in Florida was a wonderful gift to me. We returned to Massachusetts in May. The winter of 2003 had been one of the coldest on record in New England. Everyone we saw was deliriously happy when
126

the temperature reached 55 degrees. I was freezing. I had become wonderfully spoiled!

That spring, our daughter, Joan, became assistant conductor for a major symphony orchestra. We were thrilled and excited for her. Our son, Michael, after working in real estate for ten years, sold everything and bought himself a sailboat. He decided to move to the island of St. Thomas and try island life for a couple of years. Nothing makes me happier than knowing my children are happy doing what they want to do. Joan and Michael embarked on very different and individual paths, which actually allowed Larry and me to be free to explore our own lives.

I was relaxing, having a cup of tea, and catching up with "Oprah," when the telephone rang. A voice said, "Hi, this is Kyra. You do remember me, don't you?"

Once again, I was floored, surprised to hear from her again.

She started asking questions about me and Larry, and about Joan and Michael, as though we were catching up after only a few weeks apart. She said she'd missed me so much, and did I know that she loved me.

I felt a bit shell-shocked. I had heard Kyra say these very words many times before. I couldn't figure out why she was calling now.

"What are you doing tonight?" she asked.

I told her we were going to dinner with friends.

"What time will you be coming home?" she wanted to know.

Finally, I said, "What is it you're trying to ask me, Kyra?"

"Well," she said, "Phillip and I have been going through a really hard time lately. He was expelled from school for a couple of days, and I thought we could come to your house

127

tonight and stay over. Do you think we could do that?" she asked me.

I said, "It sounds really important to you to come tonight and not tomorrow."

"Yes," she continued, "and I know it sounds crazy, but we miss you guys so much and Phillip really wants to see you. You are his grandmother, you know, and I just want to know if you'd be willing to be there for us?"

I sat there with the telephone to my ear, not quite believing what I was hearing. It did sound crazy, but I didn't want to let her go. I said she and Phillip could come and stay overnight.

She asked if I'd stay up all night with her and talk.

I told her I was willing to do that, too. Meanwhile, Larry and Michael were circling around me trying to get the gist of what was being said. "Oh boy," I thought, "I have no idea what to expect from their visit."

Our friends, Brian and Mary, who were cooking dinner for us at their home, were filled with awe, as we told them about what the evening was turning into. They couldn't imagine what all of this must feel like after not hearing from Kyra for a year and a half!

At 10:30 pm, Larry looked at me and said, "They're lost. We need to go home, because they'll be calling for directions."

Sure enough, there were three messages from Kyra and Phillip on our answering machine. Larry had been correct. He called them on their cell phone and guided them to our house.

A few minutes later, Kyra pulled into the driveway. She and Phillip got out of their car, and Phillip ran and jumped into Larry's arms. "I missed you so much, Larry, and I love you!" Phillip proclaimed. Larry hugged and kissed him. When he put him down, Phillip looked at me and pointed his finger. "Are you my mother's mother?" He demanded to know.

I said, "Yes, I am," to which he responded, "Then how come you gave her away?!?"

Kyra had a black eye. "I could use a good stiff drink," she said.

CHAPTER 25
UP ALL NIGHT

Amazed is an understatement of how I felt upon their arrival. Larry made Kyra a stiff drink and told Phillip that if he'd get into his pajamas, he'd let him watch a little television before going to sleep. Phillip was all for whatever Larry suggested, so up we went to the bedroom where Phillip changed his clothes and Kyra put down her bags. I couldn't believe that this daughter of mine was actually going to sleep in one of my guest bedrooms. Larry said he'd keep an eye on Phillip so that Kyra and I could be alone.

Downstairs again, Kyra announced she was starving. I had one piece of cheese and a hamburger in my refrigerator. I hadn't been food shopping in days. We cooked it up and put it between two pieces of rye bread. She seemed happy. I could tell she was nervous, too. We settled in the living room with her sitting on the rug and me on the couch.

"Kyra," I began, "I really want to know why you disappeared again."

She looked away and down. "I have a hard time sustaining a relationship," she answered sheepishly.

I told her that it seemed to me that she thought that by disappearing, I wouldn't see her. "That might be literally true," I said, "but I see you in my mind and heart all the time." She kept looking down at the floor.

She finished her sandwich and made herself another drink. "Phillip and I have been through a lot lately," she began. "We moved to another town. I thought it would be a better school for him, but he's been getting into a lot of trouble. The social worker at his school called me into her office this week. I knew she saw my black eye, but I just ignored it and told her we were fine.

"For the past year, I've been dating a new man. I wasn't looking to meet anyone, but I met him at a bar. He started talking to me and was so sweet. I thought he was wonderful. I had been so lonely. He introduced me to cycling, and I felt like I was getting physically fit. I felt like my heart was opening in a new way. He doesn't live with us now, but he did for a while, at the place you and Larry last visited us. Things went pretty well at first, but he had a hard time with Phillip wanting to sit in between us on the couch when we watched television, or when Phillip didn't do what he asked of him. He didn't like my style of discipline and would correct me all the time. I got really nervous a couple of weeks ago when he and I were watching a movie, and the guy in the leading role said to his girlfriend, 'If I can't have you, then no one can have you!'

He looked at me and said, 'That's the way I feel about you!' It kind of scared me. Like, if I ever wanted out of the relationship, he might not let me go."

"Are you afraid of him hurting you physically?" I asked her.

"Oh, yes," she answered. "He gave me this black eye. It's not the first one he's given me, either."

I suggested she contact a group that helps women to get out of abusive relationships, but she winced at the thought. "The police were at my house yesterday," she said. "I saw them pull into the driveway. My boyfriend was in the house, and Phillip was home from school. I went outside to see what they wanted. They were really nice. They told me that the social worker at Phillip's school had called them to report about my black eye. They were checking to see if

I was all right. I told them I was, but they said that three women in the county had been murdered in the last four months by abusive boyfriends and husbands, and they had to investigate my welfare. I told them I'd be taking care of the situation, but since they were in the driveway, I was now afraid of what my boyfriend would do if they went into the house and asked him any questions. They thought about this for a minute and said they didn't want to make the situation any more dangerous than it already seemed to be. How would it be if they came into my house to talk to Phillip, since they had heard about his problems and dismissal from school? I said that would be okay. They came in and pretended they were there to check on my son.

After they left, my boyfriend looked at me and said, 'See, I told you that you don't know how to discipline that kid!' That all happened yesterday. I just had to get out of town."

I was digesting her story as best I could. It would have been easy to become outraged at how Kyra had been treated by this man, but I knew it would just inflame the situation if I inserted my feelings. I did tell her I was worried about her safety and asked if she planned on breaking up with him.

She said, "I don't exactly know what I'm going to do yet. Most of the time, he's really nice to me."

I was astonished. I was also becoming aware of how much denial Kyra had to live with in order to survive.

"You know," she said, "sometimes, I get really crazy. I mean, I can get wild and fight just like a guy."

"Does this happen in response to someone threatening you?" I asked.

"I'm not sure," she answered, "Sometimes, but other times, it feels like I just snap!"

132

We picked up her dish and glass and put them into the dishwasher. It was about one-thirty in the morning, and she was exhausted. "I really would like to go to bed now," she told me. We hugged goodnight, and she went upstairs to her bedroom. As it turned out, I did stay up all night. I curled up on the couch and reflected on the past few hours. I didn't know what to make of it all.

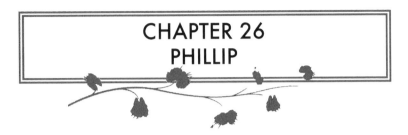

CHAPTER 26
PHILLIP

Phillip bounded down the staircase the next morning, announcing he was starving! I asked him what he would like, and he ordered bacon and eggs. He ate his breakfast with gusto.

"Wow," I said, "you were sure hungry. Do you want an English muffin?"

"Yes, I do," he responded. After his muffin and a tall glass of orange juice, he finally seemed to be satiated.

"So Phillip," I said, "what's it like to be in the first grade?"

"I'm not in the first grade," he said, "I'm in the third grade."

"Oh, but I know you're in the first. Are you just being silly?" I asked him.

"No, I'm not!" he said. "I'm in the third grade," raising his voice with emphasis.

"But Sweetheart," I continued, "I know you're seven years old and in the first grade."

He just looked at me and grinned. "I guess you got me," was his reply.

I didn't understand what he was up to. "Let's play," he suggested.

"What do you want to do?" I asked him.

With that, he announced several different outdoor games I knew nothing about. I was so out of the loop when it came to current kids' games. He was mystified at my ignorance. "How about drawing for a while," I offered. "I even have the drawing pad and crayons you used the last time you were here."

"Okay," he agreed halfheartedly.

Phillip soon announced he was bored and decided to take a walk through the house. When he returned to the kitchen, he had several items in his hands and asked if he could keep them. He had picked up small items from all over the upstairs. They weren't especially valuable, but they had been given to me as gifts from special people in my life, and I wasn't ready to let them go.

I told him that he couldn't have them. "Maybe," I said, "we could find something else for you to take home."

He seemed very surprised with my answer. And then, out of his mouth came, "Are you my mother's mother?"

Again, I answered, "Yes, I am your mother's mother."

"THEN WHY DID YOU GIVE HER AWAY?" he yelled with a scrunched-up face.

"Sweetheart," I said, "these are very adult questions you're asking me. What I can tell you is that I was too young to take care of your mommy, and your Nana and Papa adopted your mommy and raised her for me."

"Oh," he said, and walked away. Just then, Larry came down the stairs and asked Phillip if he wanted to go to Home Depot with him.

"Yeah!" he exclaimed happily. Off they went, hand in hand.

A short time later, Kyra came into the kitchen, announcing she had had one of the best night's sleeps ever. She gave me her breakfast order, and I was happy to have something to do. I told her that Phillip had asked me again if I was her mother. I wondered if this information was more than a seven-year-old could handle.

"Oh, he can handle it," she told me. "He's my little man."

Kyra confessed that she had finally told her family about reuniting with me. She said her father hadn't seemed especially interested, but her adopted brother, who had married an adopted woman, was very curious. He had been happy for her.

I talked to her about the problems Phillip was having in school. Some of his issues seemed very serious to me, but Kyra thought that going to summer camp would straighten out things. Meanwhile, however, he was struggling with reading, he was not getting along well with his classmates, and he had been accused of stealing. He was already saying that he hated school.

Kyra told me that I'd never know how much it had meant to her that I had said yes to their coming the night before. Again, she remarked that she thought our home was so peaceful, like no other home she'd ever been in. "I don't know why," she said, "but I feel happy here."

Soon, Larry and Phillip came laughing through the door, holding their packages from the store. Phillip was happy to see his mom up and eating her breakfast. "What are we going to do now?" he asked her.

"Oh Phillip, we're just going to relax and enjoy our time here," she told him.

"But I'm bored!" he yelled.

I remembered the returned Christmas packages in the front hall closet. "Hey, you two," I said, "I have something that just might save the day!"

I went to the closet and pulled out the boxes, one for Phillip and one for Kyra. I had purchased a sweater for her, and for him, I had chosen a book and a Lego kit that depicted one of the Harry Potter settings. Phillip seemed positively thrilled and asked Larry to help him put it together. The Pied Piper helped the little boy to settle down.

Kyra thanked me and said that the gifts I'd been sending her the past few years were the most beautiful gifts anyone had ever given her. There seemed to be no awkwardness for her about the fact that I had just pulled these gifts out of the hall closet. Stamped on them was "Return to Sender" from eighteen months back.

After helping Phillip, Larry told us he had to go to a business meeting and needed to say his good-byes. Phillip was very upset with this news and jumped up and down while holding onto Larry's leg. It was obvious that the boy adored him. Many hugs and kisses later, as Larry was leaving, Kyra leaned over and whispered into his ear, "I'll send you the money I owe you next week!"

CHAPTER 27
SAD LITTLE BOY

I told Phillip and Kyra I'd like to take them to lunch, and they thought it was a good idea. Kyra went upstairs to shower and dress, and Phillip followed me to my room and watched while I made my bed. As I walked into my bathroom, he started to yell at the top of his lungs, "WHY DID YOU GIVE MY MOMMY AWAY? WHY DID YOU GIVE MY MOMMY AWAY? YOU HAD HER FOR SEVEN WHOLE DAYS, AND YOU FED HER AND CHANGED HER. WHY DID YOU GIVE MY MOMMY AWAY?" This little boy was in a very agitated state.

I bent down to Phillip and put my hand under his chin to steady him. I said, "Phillip, I was too young to take care of your mommy, and that's why I had to give her away to your Nana and Papa. I don't want you yelling at me again. We can talk about this. You don't need to point your finger at me in anger. Do you understand me?" I asked firmly.

"Yes," he said, finally in a little boy's voice. After that, he went outside to play in the yard, while his mother and I got ourselves ready to go out for lunch.

Clearly, this boy was overwhelmed by the story of my having given his mother up for adoption. Kyra had shared all of the information and details of her birth, and subsequent release for adoption, with her seven-year-old child. He couldn't comprehend how I could have given his mother away. That was hard enough for me to live with. His young mind was swirling with questions. I felt it was too much for a seven-year-old to hold, let alone process.

As I came downstairs, I could see Phillip outside, throwing stones at the house.

Astonished, I asked him to stop what he was doing.

He looked at me as if to say, "What's your problem?" and kept on throwing the stones.

Kyra soon appeared, looking pretty and rested. As we were gathering our keys, we heard a car alarm. We looked outside to see Phillip in his mother's car.

"Oh my God!" yelled Kyra, running to the car. "Phillip, Phillip, how do I turn off the alarm? You're the only one who knows how to do it!"

"You do this, Mom," he answered confidently. And I watched the seven-year-old boy give clear instructions to the thirty-eight-year-old woman.

When the alarm stopped, Kyra grabbed Phillip, hugging and kissing him, saying, "Oh, thank you, Phillip, for shutting off the alarm. What would I ever do without you?" Nothing was said about the fact that he had gotten in the car and tried to start it, which had caused the alarm to go off in the first place. I couldn't wait to get to the restaurant.

We went to a local pizza place that had lots of meals for kids and also had a liquor license. I ordered a Diet Coke, and Kyra ordered a glass of wine. I was envious. Lunch seemed like a perfect time to start drinking. We found something on the menu that Phillip liked. Things seemed to be going pretty well when suddenly, Phillip shouted again, "WHY DID YOU GIVE MY MOTHER AWAY?"

"Oh Phillip," Kyra chided, "let's talk about something else."

I looked down at the placemat, and it had an outlined map of Italy. On the table was a tin of crayons for kids to use, and I suggested we color. "Phillip," I began, "I'm going to Italy in the fall."

Phillip shrieked, "Take me with you. I want to go with you!"

Kyra began to get upset with him and ordered him to simmer down and behave. She looked at me and said, "I haven't had one minute's peace in seven years!" Then she downed her wine.

I left a very generous tip for our server. I can only imagine what he thought was going on at our table. I remember hoping that someone—anyone I knew in my world—would come to the restaurant and see us. I would gladly have introduced Kyra and Phillip, if only to have a witness to the ongoing scene in our booth.

Phillip slid to the floor under the table. Kyra seemed relieved, as though just having him out of sight gave her enough space to talk, even though he was only a foot away. She was fully able to talk to me while Phillip was throwing a temper tantrum. She seemed accustomed to living in chaos.

I wanted to "stop the movie" and shout, "Do you realize this little boy seems disturbed? Do you realize that you act as though his behavior is normal? Do you realize that your behavior seems bizarre to me?"

But I didn't say anything. I paid the bill and began to gather my belongings. Phillip jumped up from under the table with a smile. "Look at what I found!" It was a dime.

"Oh, Phillip, good for you," replied his mother.

"Want to see me throw it up and catch it?" he asked.

"No," I said. "We're in a restaurant."

At the same time, Kyra said, "Sure I do! You know, Kris, he has a great arm in baseball."

"Okey dokey..." I thought.

Phillip said in a soft voice, "I want to stay at Kris and Larry's house."

Kyra replied, "So do I, Phillip, but we have to go home now."

When we got back to the house, Phillip ran inside and locked the door, leaving his mother and me outside. Kyra shouted for him to let us in, but he ignored her. I looked through the glass in the door. He was hiding under a table, trying not to be seen. I had another key, fortunately, but it was clear this little boy didn't want to leave, and he didn't mind getting into trouble with the adults in his life. He was quite experienced at being yelled at and having angry adults correcting his behavior. It seemed to roll off him.

Finally, they packed up their car for the return trip home. "Phillip, thank Kris for having us," his mother instructed him.

He hugged me and said he wanted to stay. I hugged and kissed him, telling him we'd see each other soon. They got into their car and waved and blew kisses to me as they drove down the driveway. It was as though the previous sixteen hours were as normal as eating apple pie. I was exhausted. I didn't know where to begin in sorting out my feelings.

CHAPTER 28
THE ELEPHANT IN THE ROOM

When Larry came home that night, we talked and talked about our experiences with Kyra and Phillip. We felt overwhelmed with what appeared to be major problems in their lives. In the end, we agreed that all we could do was be available when they needed someone to listen. If Kyra wanted our help or advice, we'd be happy to give it, but we couldn't tell her what to do or how to live.

I received a beautiful card from her, thanking me for a wonderful visit. "It was just what Phillip and I needed," she wrote.

I decided that corresponding by email might be a way for Kyra and me to foster a deeper relationship. I suggested that we ask whatever questions we had about each other and possibly share what was on our minds, which could give insight into who we really were. I did ask how the situation with her boyfriend was going. I wondered if she had thought any more about leaving him. And, of course, I asked about Phillip.

She said nothing in her reply about her boyfriend, and never did again. She told me that Phillip had gotten into trouble at school and was being suspended once more. Also, she had gotten into trouble at work because she'd left her shift in order to pick him up. "It's as though we were both suspended today," she wrote.

I felt so sorry for her. I told her that being a single mother must be the toughest job in the world, and that I hoped she was taking care of herself. She wrote again to say she had made an appointment with a mental health clinic. "I can't help Phillip by myself," she told me. I wrote and congratulated her on the courage it must have taken to ask for help for her son.

In the next email, Kyra told me that she had skipped the appointment at the mental health clinic. Phillip and she had decided to go to the beach instead. "That way," she informed me, "Phillip got to go to Phillipland, and I got to put in my CD earphones, listen to some music, and block him out."

I wrote back and said that I realized it was hard to face problems. I shared with her about a friend of mine who had only recently been able to talk about early childhood traumas, which had affected her entire life. They had caused her not to trust others with her story. This friend was only beginning to be able to ask for the help she needed to attain a healthy emotional life.

Kyra wrote back angrily, "Don't you ever compare me with someone else. I'm my own person. In case you don't know it, I'm a very deep person. I'm a wonderful mother, and I'm very proud of how I'm raising my son!"

Wow, she sure told me off. I began my next email expressing my surprise at her taking offense. I had thought it was the kind of story that all of us could relate to. I certainly could relate to it. "However," I said, "if I have offended you somehow, I apologize."

I was beginning to realize that not speaking my mind with Kyra from the beginning was backfiring. I had held all of my observations and questions inside, trying to be compassionate and patient, trying to understand how she felt as an adopted daughter, trying to understand what hardships she had experienced with her adopted family, and trying to understand what it was like to be a single mother, something I clearly had not been. I needed to balance the decks with Kyra and let her know where I was coming from.

When I wrote again, this is what I shared: "Kyra, when we were first reunited, I was relating to you as an eighteen-year-old girl, somehow emotionally frozen in time, and I was very scared. When I first spent time with you, I was filled with disbelief and could hardly speak. I had gone from having had you as a baby to meeting you as a thirty-three-year-old woman. All those years, you were a baby to me. I didn't know what to make of the grown-up you.

"It wasn't easy allowing you to say anything you felt like saying to me, which at times, I experienced as rude or bold. I kept excusing you, feeling that you needed to see how far you could go with me. I thought you might have some real anger about my giving you up for adoption. I've wondered if your finding me living a life that is wonderful, affluent, and filled with love may actually make you angry. You feel as though this should be your life.

"I take full responsibility for having had you and giving you up for adoption. There is pain in that for both of us. What I don't take responsibility for is your upbringing and how you feel about yourself today. That responsibility lies with your parents. I am no longer working out of my teenage frame of reference. I am working out of my wisdom place, which I have earned as a fifty-plus-year-old woman. It is from this place that I am willing to get to know you. It is up to you if you want to know that woman.

"You came to my home in crisis because of a dangerous relationship with your boyfriend. And your little boy was clearly upset with the chaos he lived in. Expecting me to witness all of this, and then being offended when I asked about your well-being, doesn't work with me. That's not
144

who I am. I don't live in chaos, and I don't plan to allow it to invade my life without naming it and doing something about it. I can't live with an 'elephant in the room' atmosphere where the shit smells to high heaven, and be expected to act as though everything is fine. If you want to know me, this who I am. It's up to you to decide."

Kyra wrote back several days later. She never referred directly to anything I said in my email to her. She told me that she had loved her mother very much, but at times, it had been hard being her daughter. She admitted to doing many things recreationally, and that now it was hard to live without them. She just wanted to be a good mother, she told me.

I didn't hear from Kyra for a long time after that. Then one day, when Larry and I returned home from a trip, we checked our email, and there was a message from her. She wrote that she was very angry with me. If she was to be perfectly honest, she informed us, she liked Larry more than me. On the other hand, I had been everything she had ever dreamed about as a child when wondering who her birth mother was. She didn't refer to anything I had previously written. She made it clear that she was a good mother and a very deep person, and wondered if I had a hard time with that. She ended by expressing her doubts that we could ever be close.

I was real with Kyra. I told her my truth. She probably had no idea how much it had cost me. But, I can honestly say that speaking to her from a place of authenticity was really what I had to give her. Somehow, this time, I was okay in the "not-so-okayness" of Kyra's absence in my life. Kyra had her own path to follow, and I honored that.

However, her message was crushing. I cried with Larry. I had given her up as an infant, and now I felt like I was having to give her up again. It seemed like too much to bear. But it also felt crazy…like I was in a maze and not sure which way to go to be free. The chaplaincy training and counseling I had received was telling me that this relationship was very unhealthy…for me…and for my family. I began to let go of any expectations I had about having a close relationship with Kyra. I needed to take care of myself.

CHAPTER 29
THE REAL SECRET

Writing my story hasn't been easy. I spent several editions getting to a place where I felt I could share it with family and friends. What I wasn't prepared for, however, was the impact I would feel over what I had intentionally not written: *I'd made the conscious decision not to write about Kyra's paternity. It was too painful.*

Then one day, after writing what I had thought was my final draft, I felt a "shift." I saw Maya Angelou appearing on "Oprah," speaking about her book, *Hallelujah! The Welcome Table.* It's about a "lifetime of memories with recipes." She was sharing with Oprah the origin of her recipe for banana pudding. She told the story about visiting a young man she was romantically interested in twice a week for sex: how she always felt better when she left than when she arrived, and how she discovered another woman with this young man on her appointed day. Even more upsetting to her was the discovery that the young man had offered her a piece of banana pudding the other woman had made for him. Indignant, she never returned. Instead, she made herself a better banana pudding than the runny one the other woman had made.

I stared at Maya Angelou. She was laughing, and the audience was laughing. She was so fine with herself. In that moment, I knew I had never been fine with myself in that easy way of just smiling and telling everyone how it was. She had visited that young man she had a romantic relationship with for sex. She could say to millions of people that she felt better when she left than when she'd arrived. She was openly discussing a topic that could have kept her covered in shame. People loved her authenticity, as did I.

I realized in that moment that I, however, couldn't claim my own authenticity until I could talk about Kyra's father. I had to tell my true story.

I was eighteen. My boyfriend was twenty-two and Jewish. I had been dating him for two years. After I moved away from my high school town, I frequently took a train back to spend time with him. With the help of his family, he had opened a diner.

On one visit, I knew the minute I walked into the diner that something had changed. I saw how the waitress was looking at him, and I knew that he was seeing her behind my back. I accused him of cheating on me, and he admitted it. We broke up.

A week later, a high school friend invited me to visit her in college. I was thrilled to be asked and excited to go. When I arrived at the college, my friend greeted me with the news that she had the measles and was quarantined to her dorm room. "Don't worry," she told me. "My boyfriend has a friend who will take you to all the parties and events this weekend. You'll have a great time." He was Portuguese. He was the captain of the football team. He took me to everything. He took me to bed.

Three days later, my body exploded with feelings I wanted to deny. "This cannot be what I think it is," I thought. I was terrified. The unthinkable happened: I missed my period.

I called the football player and told him I thought I was pregnant. He said, "You're not going to pin that one on me!" He hung up. I stood there with the telephone in my hand, listening to the dial tone. I didn't know what to do.

I called my old boyfriend and told him I had missed my period. "I don't want to marry you," he said.

"I don't want to marry you, either," I told him.

"Maybe I can find a way to get you an abortion," he offered.

"No," I told him. "I want help to have this baby." And he did help me. He paid for my stay in New York and for all my medical expenses.

I felt steely inside when I called my old boyfriend. I knew it was wrong. I told myself I couldn't be sure that he wasn't the father of the baby I was carrying. I told myself that for years. Much later, when I began working with Alysia, I was able to admit to myself and her that the other boy had fathered my child.

Deciding to find Kyra compelled me to tell the whole truth to Larry, Joan, and Michael—and to Kyra when we met that first day. She had been raised in a Jewish family, because I had said her father was Jewish. When I told her about the football player, she said, "Now I know why I've been such a good athlete." She never mentioned it again.

I never spoke to the football player or the old boyfriend again. I tried, years later, to contact them both to let them know the true story about Kyra's birth. I felt that the football player should know he fathered a child, and the old boyfriend deserved to know that he didn't father a child—something he had to live with his whole life. I hired a detective to track them both down, but was unable to find either of them. Several years ago, after my failed attempts at finding them, I prepared a ritual wherein I wrote letters to both of these boys. In the letters, I asked for understanding and forgiveness for what I had done to survive as a terrified teenaged girl. I burned the letters in a fire, and let the feelings of guilt go.

Originally, writing my story shined much light on my life. What I had left out, however, stared back at me with such force that I was broken open again. I thought that since I had told Kyra and my family the truth, I had freed myself of my enormous shame over lying about the birth-father. By not writing the whole truth—by not writing about Kyra's birth-father—I continued, however, to be enveloped in a forty-one-year-old pain-field of shame.

When I witnessed Maya Angelou's freedom to be herself, I realized that I hadn't freed myself. Never had I been so stopped in my tracks, so silenced. Nothing was the same for me after I had this realization. I could go out socially and appear fine, all the while knowing my inner world had exploded. It felt like freefall.

Larry asked, "What can I do for you?"

"Nothing," I told him.

I felt as though the train I had been riding in had ground to a screeching halt. I was left in silence. I would wake up in the morning and say to myself, "Hello, are you there? Am I here? Where am I?" I took long walks. I didn't sleep for weeks. I met with close friends and shared what was happening to me, and what had happened to me. They were kind. I wept easily.

It took the better part of a summer to feel myself come to a place where I wasn't shaking inside. I was beginning to know what it had cost me to carry the burden of my past. I knew that I did what I did to survive.

In order to thrive, however, I needed to forgive myself and live outside the drama of my story.

After a long summer of transformation, I began to get my bearings. I had awakened to an inner presence of renewal and healing. Then one day, I returned home after a long walk to hear a message on my answering machine.

"Hi Kris, it's Kyra. How is everybody? I know you probably don't want to speak to me, but I want to apologize for how inconsiderate I've been. I really love you and have a lot to tell you, if you're willing to call me back. I'll understand if you don't. I'm sorry for how I've treated you."

It had been twenty-five months since I had heard from her. I was surprised, again. I remember saying out loud, "Oh, shit; I feel something!" I cared. I had practiced not caring what Kyra was up to. It was too painful. Now she was popping back into my life again. I needed time to think about returning her call. I needed to set some ground rules. We played telephone tag for a week but finally set a time to talk.

She was right. She had a lot to tell me. "Kris," she began, "I admit I have pushed people away and isolated my life because of alcohol and drugs. Every time someone good comes along, I invariably ruin the relationship. You and Larry have been so unconditional with your love for me and Phillip, and I've treated you badly. I've had a lot of time to think of who you and Larry have been to me, and I am very sorry for my behavior. It's my behavior that I want to tell you about.

"Last March, I was stopped for driving under the influence. Soon thereafter, I lost my job and was evicted from my apartment. My life went downhill fast. I had to move Phillip and myself to subsidized housing where we're living on assistance. It's horrible here. The move was terrible. I was exhausted. I knew the movers probably had some cocaine on them. When I asked them, they gave me some. It got me through. I know I shouldn't have, but I couldn't help myself.

"A few days later, after emptying boxes and making up Phillip's room, I decided we needed a night out. We went to a nice little Italian restaurant. I swear I only had one glass of wine, but I admit I was still taking pain pills. I've been taking painkillers ever since I gave birth to Phillip nine years ago. When I was pregnant, I gained almost a hundred pounds, and the extra weight caused a herniated disk in my back. It was unbelievably painful. I've had the same doctor since I had Phillip. He's always refilled my prescriptions.

"Anyway, I guess the combination of pills and a glass of wine made my driving erratic. I was stopped by the police. They arrested me and put me in the police car. I went wild when they handcuffed me. Phillip had to witness all of it. The Department of Children's Services was called in and almost took Phillip away. I begged and begged for them to come and see that I had a good home for him. They agreed and drove me home. After inspecting the place, they allowed Phillip to remain with me. But now that I had my second DUI in six months, I lost my license for three years and was sent to jail for sixty days.

"Are you okay, Kris? I know this is a lot to tell you all at once. I could call you back tomorrow if it's too much for you."

I told her I was fine, although so much news was dizzying. I said it was okay to continue. I admit, I was beginning to take notes.

"Well," she continued, "it gets worse. Before I tell you the next episode, I want you to know that I'm completely off the pills. A couple of weekends ago, I went cold turkey. It was the most horrible experience I've ever had. I thought I'd go crazy. Half way through the first day, I tore up the entire house looking for a pill. And you know what, Kris? I found one, and I took it. I don't think I could have made it if I hadn't had that one pill.

"The week before I went cold turkey, I had a respiratory infection and needed an antibiotic. I called my doctor and requested that he call in a prescription. I also asked for my pain pills to be refilled. Since I can't drive, a friend who was coming to dinner stopped at the pharmacy to pick up my scripts. After he asked for them, there was a delay, and the next thing he knew, he was being questioned by the police.

"It seems the pharmacist on duty thought the amount of pain pills was suspiciously high. He called the doctor's office to see if they had called that prescription in. The nurse said, 'No, the office had not called that prescription in.' The pharmacist called the police, and they were notified when someone came to pick up the scripts. The next thing I knew, there was a warrant out for my arrest.

"Kris, I swear to you that I didn't call in that prescription. I'm glad we're talking today, because this afternoon I have to turn myself in. I don't know if they're going to hold me or not. I can't go back to jail. It was so horrible. Right now, talking to you, I'm standing in my back yard. Just to see blue skies and green grass is wonderful. To be able to go to the bathroom alone is amazing. This charge is a felony. If I'm convicted…I can't even go there."

"Who took care of Phillip when you were in jail?" I asked her.

"Would you believe I had to ask the boyfriend I had when I first met you to come and take care of him? He was the only person who would help me. My father doesn't speak to me. I haven't seen him in a couple of years. It was horrible calling from jail. I knew that my old boyfriend was drinking sometimes when I called. But I have to tell you, Kris, that he was wonderful to Phillip. He loves him like a son. He got him off to school every day and went to all of his games. On the weekends, he'd take him to his lake house, and they would go boating and swimming. I am very

153

grateful to him. Did I tell you that Phillip is doing great in school? And you wouldn't believe how handsome he is!"

"Have you considered going to Alcoholics Anonymous?" I asked her.

"I don't like AA," she replied. "I'm going to participate in a Mothers Against Drunk Driving program. But I don't want to attend meetings."

While Kyra was talking, I could hear the sound of a man's voice as he approached her. "No," I heard her say, "You can't go in and watch movies with Phillip."

I could hear arguing.

"Okay," she said, "I just don't want any trouble with your wife. She was all drugged up the other night, and I don't want her over here involving us." I could hear the man promise that his wife was sleeping and that there would be no trouble from her. Apparently with Kyra's permission, he went inside and watched movies with Phillip.

"Sorry for the interruption, Kris," she continued. "Last Saturday night, that man who you heard talking to me was in a big fight. They live across the street from us. His wife was hopped up on drugs, and he couldn't calm her down. Someone called the police because of the ruckus. I didn't even realize what was going on until the police cars came blazing down the street. Meanwhile, Phillip was outside throwing his ball against the house. The ball veered off and hit the door of the arriving police car. The cop inside thought someone was throwing rocks at him. He got out of his car with his gun drawn and pointed at Phillip. People were screaming that he was just a kid playing with his ball, and the officer put his gun away. I found out later that Phillip asked my neighbor if the police were coming to arrest his mother."

Kyra was right. There was a lot to process. She told me a girlfriend was driving her to the police station to surrender. She said she would have her friend call me if she was detained; otherwise, she would call that night to let me know she was okay.

Kyra's life was filled with chaos and drama. There was nothing I could do to help her.

I was grateful to hear from her later that evening. "They booked me," she said. "It wasn't a big deal. I've been photographed and fingerprinted before. The next step is waiting to hear about a court date. I do have a law firm that has helped me in the past with custody of Phillip and my DUIs, but I don't know if they're up to representing me in this case. I am being charged with impersonating a doctor, which is a felony."

I told her I was glad she hadn't been held in jail. At least I could sleep that night knowing she was home in her own bed. I told her if she wanted to, she could call me again and share whatever was going on in her life. She seemed genuinely grateful for my offer and promised to call me soon. She thanked me again for listening to her.

I realized I would never be able to mother Kyra in a traditional way. But now, I had a sense that I could still mother her in my willingness to listen and not judge. I felt at peace with this new understanding of our relationship.

Kyra called a week later. "Hi Kris, I told you I'd call. You won't believe where I'm calling you from. I'm having dinner at my boyfriend's house with his parents. I've stepped outside to call you on my cell phone. I had so much to tell you last week that I didn't tell you about Eddie. Kris, would you believe that his father is Portuguese and his mother is Irish? You do remember what you told me, don't you?" It had been seven years since our first meeting when I'd told her about her father's lineage.

"Yes, Kyra," I said. "I do remember what I told you."

"I want you to know that he's wonderful and he loves me so much. He's renovating a house and wants me and Phillip to move in with him. I think I'm going to do it."

I was still digesting the Portuguese/Irish connection. I didn't know what to think about her moving in with Eddie. We ended our conversation with her telling me she wanted to see me face to face, look into my eyes, and tell me she loved me. I said I needed time to think that over. I also said that if we met, we would need to be alone…no Phillip, no Larry. Just the two of us. She agreed to my terms.

A week later, she left a message on my answering machine saying that she was going to Florida with Eddie. Eddie wanted to meet her father. She called several days later to tell me that Eddie had met with her father, although her father had refused to see her. So Eddie, on his own, beseeched her father to help hire an attorney who would be more savvy in a case as serious as Kyra's. If convicted, she could face up to eight and a half years in prison. She came home happy that Eddie loved her enough to do that for her. And, she was hopeful that she and her father might reconcile in the near future. She knew I would be leaving for Florida in a week, and it was important to her that she see me before I left.

We tried several times to fix a time to meet. She needed to get a ride because of her revoked license, and that made things difficult. Eddie saw his kids from his first marriage on a certain day and wouldn't be available to drive her. They were going to be moving into the new house. Phillip had a doctor's appointment. We narrowed it down to two possible times. "I'll call you first thing in the morning," she told me. "You know I want to see you."

She never called.

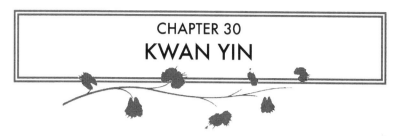

CHAPTER 30
KWAN YIN

Alysia invited me to accompany her to New York City to see His Holiness, the head of the Tibetan Bön. He was in America to teach and raise funds for the orphans living at the Menri Monastery. We stopped for lunch along the way, and I told her how sad I felt that Kyra was not communicating with me again. I felt frustrated and powerless after another one of her disappearances. Alysia suggested that there was something I could do.

She said it was true that I couldn't alter the situation, but I could put my energy elsewhere. Instead of sitting in my sadness, I could make an intention, an offering, or I could do something for another person in Kyra's name and help someone else who wanted to be helped. That way, the energy around my frustration and helplessness wouldn't become stagnant and feed into my sense of hopelessness about my relationship with Kyra. I had the power to move the field by doing something that could make a difference. In other words, if Kyra wasn't able to receive my love, then for goodness' sake—give it to someone who could! This was a revolutionary new idea to me.

When we arrived at the residence where His Holiness was staying, I was nervous and excited to be introduced to him. It was because of my relationship with Alysia that I would have the honor of a private meeting with this holy man. Our names were called, and we were invited into the room with His Holiness and several other lamas. We were given his blessing and sat down to talk with him. Alysia had many, many things to tell him, as did he to her, and I was happy just listening.

His Holiness showed us a huge stack of pictures of the many improvements at the monastery. He proudly showed the smiling, happy faces of the children at the orphanage. As he was sharing, he showed us a picture of a young woman and told us that her life was very, very difficult. She had come to the monastery looking for help. There was a sponsorship fund in place for the orphans, but nothing in place for a case like this. Alysia looked at me and said, "Well Kris, this is an opportunity to move the field around your pain with Kyra. It seems Spirit is presenting you with an opportunity to help someone. Do you want to do this?" she asked.

I said, "Yes!" I've been Yangchen's sponsor ever since that day.

It marked the beginning of my understanding about the possibility that *pain and suffering can be transformed, and that I have the power to do it.* Instead of being chained by my losses and regrets, I discovered that I can find purpose in them. *My experiences become grist for the mill, ground to the finest grains of truth.* I realized that *truth is never going to kill me, but that secrets and lies can.* Telling my story gave me the power to transform what had seemed like incredible loss into self-realization. I couldn't be who I am today without having lived what I have lived. *I don't need happy endings. What I need is to live my life authentically while allowing truth to surface in all that I do and say. I am no longer voiceless. I am no longer speechless.*

From the first day I met Alysia, I was fascinated by the statue in her studio of an Asian woman sitting atop a lotus flower. "Who is that?" I asked her.

"She's Kwan Yin, the Goddess of Compassion. She carries the tears of the world," she told me.

"Ah," I said, "I've never heard of her."

As our work continued to deepen, Alysia asked me, "Kris, do you know your mother loves you?"

"Well, it's hard for me to feel that," I said.

"I don't mean your earthly mother, Kris; I mean your Divine Mother."

"Divine Mother," I exclaimed, "I have no idea what you're talking about."

Raised as a Roman Catholic, the Blessed Mother, Mary, was the closest to divine a female could come that I could imagine. The Church, however, had always been clear in its teaching that Mary was not divine. So no, I couldn't conceive of the idea that I had a Divine Mother.

"Someday, you will," Alysia assured me.

But I felt very skeptical. At the time, I couldn't have found a loving feeling about my mother if I tried.

As my work continued, my tears spilled and spilled, and all the time I was remembering what Alysia had told me about having a Divine Mother. I couldn't feel her. It took years before I felt my heart melting, and I experienced being liberated from my childhood suffering. Compassion surfaced in me in a way I had never known before. I was able to feel it towards my mother, my father, my stepfather, my siblings, my daughter, and my grandson. When I could finally feel myself, I could also feel those around me. When I could finally feel myself, I could also love those around me.

One day, I walked by a painting of Kwan Yin, and my heart leapt. Tears welled up. Ignited in me was the deep knowledge that *indeed I do have a spiritual mother. She sits atop a lotus flower.* The lotus can only grow out of the muck. I, too, went into the muck of my life. In that muck, the roots of my Mother were there with me, reminding me of the beauty that could come when I, too, could rise up and bloom.

After my introduction to His Holiness in New York, I attended a retreat he was giving in the city. I will never forget the answer he gave to a question voiced by one of the attendees: "Holiness, how do I pray?"

The Bön have a wonderful array of statues depicting the different deities, both male and female, to whom one can pray. Many of these statues surrounded the altar where His Holiness was seated. I was surprised when he said, "To pray to deity is very easy. If you want Jesus to come to you, then put him on your altar. He will come. Just ask him. Whoever you want to come to you will come to you!"

"What would happen," I thought, "if I put an image of Divine Mother on my altar and asked her to come to me?"

I had an astonishing dream. I was leading a workshop for women. I announced that we would be finding our clitorises. Some of the women were shocked at what I was saying and hurriedly gathered their things to leave. I implored them to stay. "Don't go!" I told them. "DON'T YOU WANT TO KNOW YOUR POWER?" I cried out.

When I remembered this dream the next day, I felt embarrassed by my subconscious expressing herself that way. I have never even used the word clitoris in a sentence, let alone announced that I would help someone to find hers! I sat with the metaphor the dream was giving me about the fear I had about knowing my power.

When I applied to Mount Holyoke College, I said I was willing to be a student; when I applied to become a chaplain, I said I was willing to care; when I began to tell my story, I said I was willing to feel; when I began to feel, I said I was willing to be seen; when I was seen, I said I was willing to be heard; when I was willing to be heard, I found my voice and was willing to speak my truth; when I spoke my truth, I found my power.

CHAPTER 31

YANGCHEN

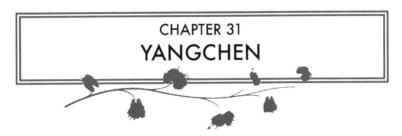

I was turning sixty years old. It was a milestone for me, because both of my parents were dead by that age. I knew life went on, of course, but since my models had died young, I couldn't imagine life beyond a certain point. So here I was at sixty, feeling great, in good health, and finally able to take a full and deep breath. I wanted to mark the occasion with something special. I didn't need a party. I wanted to do something that could make a difference.

I had continued to be Yangchen's sponsor and had heard that she was struggling with her expenses. She had become a teacher to the little nuns, called Anis, at the nunnery located on the same property as the Menri monastery. She was making thangkas, which are wall hangings depicting Bön deities usually painted on canvas. Yangchen made thangkas with a cloth appliqué technique. I decided to sponsor construction of an addition to the nunnery, which would offer school space and work space for Yangchen to teach the nuns how to appliqué, and private living quarters for her. This offer was met with much joy and gratitude, and I was invited to visit the monastery and meet Yangchen. My son, Michael, also very involved with the Bönpo and considered "family" by Lama Chongtul, was invited too to visit Menri; so we planned to travel together to Delhi.

To tell you I was excited just doesn't express how thrilled I was about this journey. It's all I thought about for months: the visa, the plane tickets, the hotel arrangements, and what to wear. We were just about to hire a driver to take us from Delhi to Menri when Lama Chongtul emailed Michael.

Lama Chongtul said he would be in Delhi at the same time and would escort us to the monastery. What an honor for us to have this holy man be our guide! We flew out of Newark, New Jersey, and took a non-stop, thirteen-hour flight to Delhi.

Sitting on the plane, curling up in my window seat, I thought about so many things. I thought about all the work I had done over the years to free myself and feel more alive. Alysia once said to me, "Kris, you may need to help lots and lots of children to fill that hole in your heart."

I think she was right. The thought that I could be helping many children filled my heart with joy. I thought about the voice work I had done with Jill Purce. Certainly her belief in the resonant fields of our families following us through our lives was true for me. Here was Michael, sitting with me on this plane, whose own story corroborated Jill's teachings. A few years before our journey to India, he had dated a woman who was eight years older than him and one day younger than the sister he still didn't know he had. He continued this pattern of dating older women for years.

One day, he brought home Annie. She was an extrovert and freely shared her family's story. She told us that her mother, married with several children, had an affair with her father. When she had become pregnant, she broke it off with Annie's father, and told her husband that Annie was his. Her husband didn't discover Annie's paternity for several years. When he did, he divorced Annie's mother, and she got in touch with Annie's biological father to tell him she was free. They married. *Wow*, I thought, *this story about women getting pregnant and telling lies to survive is going to continue to come into my life unless I free myself of its power over me.* Michael and I laugh about it these days. I told him I hoped I have cleared the resonant field enough for him to meet women with no similarities to my story.

I fell in and out of sleep with the sounds of the engines in my ears. I was passing over time zones, going towards a place I may have always been destined for. We landed at the Delhi Airport and were met by a driver from our hotel.

India was a new reality for us. Just standing and waiting for our luggage to be put into the hotel van was a sensory overload. So many people! Everywhere! The driver began our trip to the hotel, and we were assaulted by the endless honking of horns. In India, you apparently need to honk your horn at all times. There is so much in the road passing for "transportation": trucks, motorcycles, three-wheeled vehicles, a cow or two, and bicycles—all going in and out of traffic as though there are no rules, except to get where you're going and survive. I could hardly believe what I was seeing out my window. In the United States, this traffic would be considered total chaos. Before we entered the hotel grounds, we were stopped by armed guards who used bomb-detecting devices to check under our car for explosives. We were allowed to continue. A great hotel suite allowed us the rest we sorely needed. We planned to sightsee and shop a bit the next day after a good night's sleep.

The next morning, we hired a driver to take us to visit many of the popular sites in Delhi. We went to a bazaar and bought gifts for family and friends. We went to temples and leftover British army barracks. We came to a stoplight along the well-maintained road.

As we waited for the light to change, out from under an embankment came a girl about seven years old who ran to our car and banged on our windows. "RUPEES!" she yelled. I could hear her yelling even though the windows were closed. She picked up her fist and banged on the windows again. I knew she was young, because her second teeth were still coming in. Her hair was matted, and her clothes were torn and dirty. I looked at Michael, who seemed just as astonished as I was. The driver never turned around.

All of this lasted about thirty seconds. Michael and I both started to speak and look for some loose change when the light turned green and the driver drove off. The little girl ran after our car and banged it with her hand and kicked it with her feet, all the while screaming, "RUPEES! RUPEES! RUPEES!" Oh, my God! We sat in this luxury car driven by a uniformed driver, and we didn't open the window to give a rupee to a begging child. We were so bummed out by the experience that we instructed the driver to return us to the hotel. After a couple of days of rest, we met Lama Chongtul at the Delhi Railway Station and began our day-long journey up into the mountains to reach Menri.

It was wonderful to be with Lama Chongtul in India! We had always been with him in the United States where he was either traveling with His Holiness or teaching on his own. He is an extraordinary Tibetan man, a monk, a lama, a rinpoche, and a friend.

He is able to move easily between many worlds. He travels much of the time, attending to monasteries on several continents. He speaks five languages. And, he can eat anything! On the train, he offered us a lunch that he had bought at the train station. It was something wrapped in newspaper, and he relished every bite. I was sticking with my bottled water! At every stop, he got off, bought more food, and finished it all.

I asked him if he had ever heard of the expression *hollow leg.*

"No," he said.

I explained that when a person can eat and eat and eat, and never get full, it's sometimes referred to as having a "hollow leg."

He laughed and laughed. "Oh, hollow leg, I like that," he said. He had his cell phone and CD player, and was listening to songs devoted to Divine Mother. He was singing along like it was a pop tune. Besides being His Holiness's devoted aide, a teacher, and lama to thousands of people, Lama Chongtul's wish was to build a vocational school in Delhi. "It's the young people I'm worried about," he remarked. "They have no citizenship, no way to leave the country, and no way to return to Tibet. They need a vocational school so they can become independent, earn a living, and not live like refugees."

As we slowly made our way up the mountainside, I could see panoramic views of a beautiful valley to my right. The train tightly hugged the mountain on the left. Every so often, people came through the vegetation like a mirage and waved and smiled at the passengers. In one small town, the train stopped just outside the station for about twenty minutes. Looking out my window and down the tracks, I saw a woman dressed in a brightly-colored, yellow sari—holding a large basket on her head while walking towards our train. Behind her came four young children, all smiling. She appeared to be their mother. Behind the children followed a man who I assumed was their father. He was carrying a large drum. The woman put her basket down, spread a cloth on the ground beside the tracks, and motioned to her husband to sit. She was smiling like the children.

Then I saw the children jump over the tracks towards our train and joyfully receive water and newspaper-wrapped leftover food from the passengers on the train. As each child received morsels of food from the travelers, that child would run to the father and give it all to him. Then, he shared what he had with his family. When our train began to chug along again, I couldn't help being moved by the apparent joy this impoverished family had shown as they shared this meager meal. Even in poverty, the woman was beautifully dressed. I was reminded of my Chico travel wear and how masculine I looked in comparison.

Michael and I shared our experience with Lama Chongtul about the begging girl in the city who yelled RUPEES! RUPEES! RUPEES! while kicking and smacking our cab. We told him how badly we had felt, because we didn't respond to her in time. We had actually been afraid to open the window, we told him.

"Ahhhh" he said, "this happens many times to Western travelers in India. There is no right or wrong thing to do. Sometimes people open the window to the cab and give a lot of money to the person who is begging, and then that person is assaulted because other people are watching and want to steal the money."

"What do you do?" we asked him.

"Oh," he said, "I just pray."

I was lulled by the click, clack, click, clack of the train on the tracks and thought about the incredible journey I was on. I remembered the title of a book written by Maya Angelou, *Wouldn't Take Nothing for My Journey Now,* and thought that those words described where I was in my heart and spirit. It seemed that this amazing woman of wisdom appeared in my life, time and again, whenever my consciousness was rising. All of my story and everyone in it had brought me to this moment, and I wouldn't change anything. How amazing to feel this.

We arrived at Dolanji, our destination. We were met by two Lamas in an SUV and driven to the monastery. We entered the grounds by traveling on a dirt road with dust spraying everywhere. We were told that the Indian government was going to pave the road by spring because the Dalai Lama was coming for the opening of the new Bön Library. Here I was, at last, at the place I had heard so much about from so many others. I could hardly contain my excitement.

Michael and I were delivered to the guest house and shown to our rooms. We would meet with His Holiness in the morning. Until then, we had time for ourselves to rest and have an early dinner. We lingered on the balcony outside our rooms and looked out over the mountain range. We could see the nunnery off in the distance and hear children's voices as they laughed and played in the schoolyard deep in the valley. Beside us we could see the boy's dormitory, and above us and within the monastery grounds lay the Lamas' quarters and the temples. A thin mist streamed through the valley. I closed my eyes and felt like I was home.

After breakfast the following morning, Michael and I were escorted to His Holiness's quarters for tea. I realized that I had never actually been with His Holiness alone in conversation. I had always been with Alysia, who did a fair share of translating. His Holiness did speak pretty good English. It was I who was nervous.

We were brought to his quarters where he blessed us and invited us to have Tibetan tea. I drank a cup. Another was poured, and then another, when His Holiness said, "Ah, you like Tibetan tea!"

I smiled and said, "Yes," but I noticed that he wasn't drinking any. I asked him why.

He said, "Oh, the doctor won't let me because of all the yak butter in the tea. It could make me ill."

I said, "So you've give me tea with yak butter, and I might get ill?!"

"Oh no," he laughed. "You no get sick. You much younger than me."

We laughed, and the other Lamas in the room laughed, and in that instant, I knew I would be okay. No translator was needed. I felt joy in this holy man's presence.

His Holiness leaned over to his aide, and I could hear him speaking in Tibetan. All I could make out was Yangchen. He wanted to know where she was.

Outside, Lama Chongtul had come upon her and said, "Hurry up, Yangchen, don't you know your American mother is waiting for you?"

I could hear the rustling at the door, with lots of murmuring from the lamas, and then, there she was. A beautiful, petite Indian girl dressed in a beautiful sari entered the room. She had long, brown hair and wonderful, big eyes. I stood up and opened my arms to her. She looked back at me with a smile on her face, and walked into my arms. I held her close and could hear His Holiness behind me softly speaking in Tibetan to the other lamas. I could hear the love in the sounds he made. I didn't know how long to hold her. We were from very different cultures, and I didn't want to force her to stay in my big Western embrace. But, as I lightened my hold of her, I felt her arms clutch tighter around me, and I saw tears in her eyes. In that moment, the hole in my heart was filled.

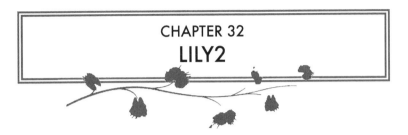

CHAPTER 32
LILY2

For fourteen years, Lily was my beloved feline friend. When she came to me as a kitten, she was the sweetest little fur ball with white ballerina paws. I could do anything with her. Every morning, I would pick her up and kiss her white belly; when I let her go, she would run off purring.

Lily had black markings on her face and back, but it wasn't until she grew bigger that I realized the black mark on her back was shaped like the letter "L." How perfect— Lily Landry had her own monogram!

Last year, she was fine at her annual checkup. But several months later, she seemed listless; she was losing weight, and her white fur was turning yellow. The vet told me she had liver cancer and that she only had a short time to live. This was devastating news to hear.

I cherished the days I had left with her, and when she passed, I thought I would never get another pet. The pain of losing her was too deep even to think about letting myself love a pet again.

For many months after Lily passed, Larry would read aloud the ads for cats up for adoption, but I would say, "No!" But he could see how lonely I was without Lily, so he persisted.

Then one day, he showed me the picture of a cat in need of adoption. She was white with black markings and part Siamese. Something in her blue eyes made my heart open. The ad said she had been rescued and that she needed to be the only pet in a home—preferably one without children.

The next day, we drove two hours to the condo where the rescuer had kept the cat in a bedroom for three months—out of reach of the rescuer's big boy cat who kept attacking the newcomer.

We learned that someone had found the skinny, terrified cat living by a gas station. When she was rescued, they discovered she had an identification chip in her, but a call to her owners revealed they had moved. While waiting for someone to adopt the abandoned cat, the rescuer named her Lily!

Somehow we managed to put this petrified animal into our pet carrier for the drive to our home, listening to her howls from the back seat all the way. Oh boy, were we naïve! We had no idea what we were in for.

Lily2 was hell on wheels! Declawed by her former owners, her first instinct was to bite, which she demonstrated on Larry during our first week. He needed a tetanus shot and an antibiotic—not to mention endured pain in his hand!

She hissed when anyone came near her. She demanded to eat all the time. As I recalled the sight of "her" bedroom back at the rescuer's condo, I now understood why there had been no less than five plates of food on the floor! Apparently the condo lady had no better luck satisfying her than I did.

Feeding time included Lily2 slamming her body into my legs and scratching them with her teeth. When she was sure she had my attention and the blood was running down to my feet, she would run to where I had put out her food and stare at me with a frantic look that said she was not yet happy with what I had offered.

Lily2 loved being brushed—but you had to do it just the right way, or her head would lurch back as though she were being attacked. When our son Michael came to care for her for a few days, he resorted to wearing an oven mitt while he brushed her!

What does Lily2 have to do with the Last Tipi? It occurred to me that Lily2 perfectly demonstrates our need to have our stories told. She arrived in my life obviously abused, abandoned, terrified, and starved. I have been witnessing the trauma of her untold story for almost a year now.

Frankly, it was her beauty that moved me even to try. At one point early on, I had decided to take her to my vet to be euthanized, for I was quite certain no one else would adopt a cat with such aggressive behavior. But I was guided to be patient. Admittedly, it has taken a lot of patience, but she is healing—and in many ways I am, too.

Lily2 told me her story with a shuddering body and fearful eyes. She needed me to understand her pain and fear. My patient "listening" is paying off: Lily2 is telling a new story these days. Her progress is quite miraculous.

In fact, she's sleeping at my feet even as I write this to you. What a transformation! When she first came to us, to my great surprise, she could sleep with her eyes open! I had never seen anything like it before—didn't even know it was possible. But right now, I can look at her blissfully closed eyes as I listen to her sweet snoring sounds.

Like Lily2, most of us have stories of abandonment, abuse, and neglect that have left us starving for our lost selves. Telling our stories sets us out on healing journeys that can bring light to those moldy places we've kept in the darkness within us. Those places of abandonment, neglect, and betrayal need healing light to help us clear space for a better story.

People who bite and draw blood and make demands usually feel unseen, unknown, and unloved. Like Lily2, they need kindness, patience, compassion, and understanding to find the courage to tell their deepest truths and to allow others to really "know" them for the first time.

I believe one reason for Lily2's remarkable progress has been the tone in my voice when I say Lily. After many years of saying the name of my beloved first Lily, I think Lily2 can feel the resonance—the loving vibration in my voice—when I say her name. And she responds to it.

Believe me, Lily2 is a very big girl now—we could just as easily have named her Attila! I share this small observation to suggest that when you are telling your story—to yourself—or to those to whom you feel safe sharing your story, that you remember it is the sound with which you say your beloved name that sets the tone for your healing journey.

AN UNEXPECTED EPILOGUE

Here is where I planned to end our journey of healing through storytelling in the last tipi. But something totally unforeseen came into my life, and I can't possibly leave the last tipi without sharing it with you.

One beautiful June day in Florida, Larry and I picked up our friends, Jack and Sheila, to go out to dinner. As they settled into the back seat of our car—attorney Jack with a phone to his ear and Sheila energetically rummaging through her purse for something—I told her, "You look like a squirrel searching for a nut!"

She laughed, "I have something for you." She handed me a crumpled clipping from the Sunday *New York Times Book Review* and said, "This might mean something to you."

I began to read the review of *Postcards From Cookie: A Memoir of Motherhood, Miracles, and a Whole Lot of Mail* by Caroline Clarke, but none of it meant anything to me—not at first.

The book's author, Caroline Clarke, is an adopted African American woman who sought medical history information from the adoption agency with which she had been placed thirty-seven years before. She discovered that her birth mother was the daughter of a prominent Hollywood figure known throughout the world—none other than the renowned singer Nat King Cole. Her memoir recounts how she connected with her birth mother, Carole Cole, also known as "Cookie," and how she had a relationship with her until her death several years before the publication of *Postcards*.

I was speechless. I read it again and again. I looked at the picture depicted on the cover of the book on that tiny piece of newsprint and it was Carole—my roommate—my dear friend with whom I had lived before giving up my baby. I had known who her family was. I didn't reveal it in *The Last Tipi* because it wasn't *my* story to tell—and it was *her* secret to keep. We had stayed in touch for more than fifteen years—a postcard here, a phone call there. But as time went on, I didn't hear from her and was unable to locate her.

Several years ago, Natalie Cole, Carole's sister, was appearing at the Kravis Center in Palm Beach, Florida. I had a card delivered to her dressing room, asking her to deliver a note I'd written to Carole, telling her I hoped we could connect one last time; but I don't know if Carole ever received it. I was truly sad to hear of her passing some time later.

All of this was flowing through me as I read the book review. Sheila was one of a few close friends with whom I had shared of my relationship with Carole. Imagine if she had never read that book review; the synchronicity was staggering!

I ordered the book. I couldn't put it down. I read into the night. Reading Caroline's words describing Carole's story threw me back in time to my own story: the Washington Square Home for Friendless Girls, 65 East 82nd Street, New York, New York—just up from Park Avenue. I didn't expect to feel so much. Caroline wrote about a package she'd received one Mother's Day from Carole that contained mementos of her time at the Washington Square Home.

Caroline recounts in the book that Carole had written in one of her mementos about her housemates and the nicknames she had for them. When I read the words, *Mo is for Maureen,* I began to cry. Caroline wondered about Cookie's housemates and what became of them.

When I finished the book, I wrote to Caroline's publicist explaining that I had been one of Cookie's housemates. Would he be kind enough to forward my attached letter to Caroline? To my surprise, he wrote right back saying it was wonderful to hear from me and that he would forward my letter to her immediately.

Caroline's Letter

Dear Caroline:

Reading the New York Times review of your book; **Postcards from Cookie**, *I was jolted back in time as the memories of your dear mother and your birth flowed unexpectedly into my view, and they have been swirling through me ever since.*

Compelled to order your book, it arrived yesterday, and I found myself reading into the night, completely transfixed with the stories you tell, knowing that I know most of them first hand. It was when I read through page 147, where you write of opening a package from Cookie labeled Washington Square Home...and I read the part about Cookie's Washington Square Home housemates, that my heart began to pound..."Mo is for Maureen." Wiping tears from my eyes, I was up all night reading. I am Maureen.

I never knew the complete name of the Washington Square Home. We were not "friendless" girls to each other. The months we spent together bonded us for life, and I had often fantasized about Millie, Barbie, Carole, and me meeting for dinner in New York and sharing what happened to our lives after giving our babies up for adoption. When I heard the news of Carole's dying, the fantasy, of course slipped away.

My baby was due Christmas Day, and you were due, I believe, a bit later. But on Christmas Day, our Carole was whisked off to Lenox Hill Hospital to give birth. On the 26th of December, we all made the pilgrimage to go and see Carole and meet you. The next day, the 27th, I awoke to labor pains and took the same walk to the hospital. When I awoke from recovery, there I was in the bed beside your mother. I saw you before I saw my own baby. There was Carole...her legs propped up and you nestled in her thighs. She couldn't stop looking at you and talking to you.

The reunion you had with Carole was beautiful, and it brought tears to my eyes for my old friend. There is a deep suffering in the sisterhood we shared, and the joy of knowing that you found each other brings happiness to my heart.

If you would like me to share more about my experiences with your mother and our "housemates," I would be happy to communicate further with you. I do not wish to intrude in your life, as you may feel completely satisfied with all you were able to share in the seven years...and seven visits...you had with each other.

I will close by sharing about the smile it brought to my lips as I learned from your writing that Carole and I both journeyed to Buddhism for comfort, that we read daily affirmations, and love to drive a Lexus. And, yes, I drink a "green drink" every day, too.

One more thing: Carole was going to be an actress, and I was going to be a singer. In 1965, I had an agent who thought Maureen Publicover was not the name of a "star." So without a thought, I changed my name to Kris Kover. Several months later, while singing with a folk group at a club in Boston, I met my husband of forty-eight years. He could never call me Maureen...so I've gone by Kris ever since.

Thank you for writing a beautiful tribute to my friend, Carole, and for sharing your challenging journey of being adopted. I also want to thank you for shining a compassionate light on how difficult it is to give up a child and how being "that" child has its own incredible journey.

Sincerely,
"Maureen" Kris Landry

Three weeks later, I found a message on my phone from Caroline Clarke saying she would love to speak to me, and thanking me for the "gift" of my letter. When we finally connected, we spoke for sixty-seven minutes. How do I know this? I think it's because of the way the mind works when something seems surreal and unimaginable. The ability to perceive on multiple levels kicks in, and I found myself listening and talking and observing and remembering.

I could see Caroline as that infant tucked into Carole's thighs, while simultaneously picturing Carole—wherever she was—smiling at the indescribable sweetness of the moment when her baby met her housemate from nearly fifty years before. Here was someone who could help fill in the gap between Caroline's actual birth and earliest baby picture at a month old. Who gets to do this?

Every cell in my body was tingling with joy and gratitude, and when the call ended, we promised to stay in touch and hopefully meet someday. I looked at my phone: We had spoken for over an hour.

Cue the violins and the angelic choir—does the cliché "full circle" come to your mind?

What a blessed way for me to leave the last tipi. My story has been told. I've looked at secrets and lies, and through telling my truth, have found my power. I've looked at everything I dared not look at, and I have lived through it all. I have left behind what no longer serves me, and I have transformed that lost young girl's guilt and despair into a realization of the utter perfection of my story.

My story has informed me of my power and courage, my willingness to crack open secrets that previously kept me trapped in a prison of my own making. It let me take the breathtaking plunge into knowing who I am and why I am here.

It's so simple, really. I'm here to share this last tipi story with you, and to extend an invitation to courageously tell your old story—the good, bad, and ugly—in the last tipi, so you can make room for your continuing, new and improved story. May your journey heal you in ways never imagined!

Kris & Caroline Meet - February, 2015.

PART 2
—
YOUR STORY:
DISCUSSION GUIDES

WHY CREATE DISCUSSION GUIDES?

The voice on the phone struggled to keep tears at bay, as she told me she had spent the afternoon and evening reading my manuscript. "I've been afraid to read it," she told me. "I've put it off for weeks, but today I was alone, so I climbed into bed, under the covers, and I just finished it. I am so moved—because I *have* written my story, but now I realize I have never gone into the last tipi, and I want to know how!"

It's because of the question posed to me, and other readers asking that same question, that I thought some guidance might be of help. I was encouraged to create discussion guides for others to enter the last tipi and tell their stories. "It would be so great if people had help on how to write their stories and open themselves to the healing you experienced," I was told.

At first, I thought I'd offer these guides separate from my story—to help people tell their own stories or those of their loved ones. After I finished writing the guides, however, I realized that they needed to be included *with* my story. My desire is that everyone who reads my story has a chance to write their own or help someone else!

I've divided Section 2 into three discussion guides. The first guide helps you tell your story. The second guide helps you assist a loved one in telling a story. The third guide helps you tell the story of someone who has passed. So here we go!

DISCUSSION GUIDE 1
WRITING YOUR STORY

I didn't start out to write a book. Outside of my chaplaincy program, I had no experience with writing. When friends would encourage me to write about my life, hoping I would share my story, I thought to myself: *I'm not a writer. I've never taken a writing course. How could I possibly do this?* And the thought of going public with my story seemed crazy to me. I simply couldn't imagine it.

It's possible that you are also in the place of not imagining how you could write or even tell your story. I realize you could buy a hundred books on "how to write your story," and they would all be good. But in this first guide, I will share with you where I was along the way as I dared to unfold the stories of my life. I hope you will be inspired to let go and release what stories you are holding that may no longer serve you—so you may write or tell a newer, better story some day.

Following are twelve lessons to help you uncover your story—including examples from my writing experience and exercises to get you started. Please use the space provided or your own notebook or voice recorder so you can document what you were thinking and feeling as you reflected on these questions. Your answers may become the seeds for your written story!

LESSON 1
WRITE YOUR STORY FOR YOU!

Thinking about other people reading your work can be distracting. Write the way you speak. Have a conversation with yourself. Just be real. Let go of the mindset, "I'm not a writer. I can't spell. I don't know grammar." Pretty soon, you've talked yourself out of writing anything. If you aren't comfortable writing, try talking your story out and recording your answers. Breathe!

When I first sat down, I stared at a blank page for quite a while. Where will I begin? What part of my life am I going to write about? My advice is to start SOMEWHERE, ANYWHERE! You can always go back and change things around. Just begin!

Lesson 1 Exercise

- What is top of mind when you consider what topic you want to write about for your life story? Spend a few minutes reflecting on this question, and then write what comes to mind.

_____

_____

_____

_____

_____

LESSON 2
KEEP AT IT

Set a goal of writing a paragraph a day to ensure that progress is being made. This paragraph doesn't have to be looking for a Pulitzer Prize. It's simply an opening…to you.

I began to write a sentence or two and then a paragraph or two. When I would go back another day and read what I had written, it seemed to become clearer to me what I was trying to say. Sometimes I'd erase what was there and begin again, because the juices got going and words started spilling out that better described what I was feeling.

Lesson 2 Exercise

- Regarding the topic you uncovered in Lesson 1, what comes to mind to write about? Don't worry about what comes first, second, or last in your story. Just write a paragraph each day. If you can't access the words to describe your desired topic, write about whatever is on your mind at that moment to get the juices flowing.

_____

_____

_____

_____

LESSON 3
BE A STORYTELLER FIRST, A CRITIC LAST

Don't get stuck expecting perfection; just tell your story. Are you writing a memoir? This word scared me, because it seemed to hold so much expectation of me to be a good writer. Judgment! You're just telling your story. Breathe, and keep it simple.

I attended a workshop for people writing their memoir. It was inspiring, because I realized many people had a story to tell. And it was a bit terrifying because there was audience feedback. I left thinking that my story was my story, and it was enough. If I needed help organizing my thoughts later, I could always find someone to edit my work.

Lesson 3 Exercises

- What limitations hold you back from writing your story?

- What fears stand in your way?

- What resources or people could help you in areas

- Where you might be less strong (like editing, marketing, publishing)?

LESSON 4
MAKE YOUR KEY CHARACTERS 3D

You could begin by telling about your family of origin... mother, father, siblings, where you were born, etc. These all become characters in your story. Think about a novel you have read and how in depth the characters were developed and described.

When I did this, I had no idea where it would take me. It seemed like I was just listing facts. I had no feelings I could actually feel. But I kept plugging along, and pretty soon I had the makings of the story of my early childhood. As I read it back to myself, I realized how those early days had affected my adult life.

Lesson 4 Exercises

- What key characters influenced your childhood?

- Young adulthood?

- Midlife?

- Current life?

Describe each one physically, and explain what influence each had on your life.

LESSON 5
MOVE THROUGH FEAR

Don't be afraid to write about the difficult times. Almost everyone has some unresolved issues from childhood. Write everything you remember…your age…the time of the year…colors and smells.

I was surprised at what came up when I wrote about my brother, who had been institutionalized as a small boy because he was developmentally challenged. My mother told me never to speak of him. When I started writing about my memories of him, I was flooded with feelings I didn't know I had. It was after writing about my brother that I got the inspiration to find him and be with him for the first time in more than forty years.

Lesson 5 Exercises

- What is the hardest event(s) you have experienced? Describe it in detail.

- Have you ever expressed this to anyone before?

- What "secrets" do you have?

Realize you don't have to include these events in your public story unless you choose to do so, but sometimes until writing them, you won't know what needs to be included.

LESSON 6

BUILD YOUR RELATIONSHIPS

Develop your characters and the relationship you had with them. What was your relationship with your parents, siblings, family members, friends from school? Your memories may all be good ones, or perhaps you remember secrets you had to keep or feelings you couldn't express.

When I think back about my mother now, I have deep compassion and empathy for her. She felt the need to institutionalize her son and raised me as a single parent for ten years. She wasn't physically well and was emotionally drained. When I think of her today, I am amazed at what she did for me as a child. But as that child, I felt disconnection, fear, and abandonment. Because I allowed myself to write about my early life and feel so many repressed feelings, I am now at peace with my relationship with my mother.

Lesson 6 Exercises

- Regarding the characters you listed in Lesson 4, what limitations did they experience?

- How did their limitations affect your life?

- What emotions do you have towards each of these characters today?

- How do those emotions differ from what you may have felt years ago?

- Why have the emotions changed, if they have?

LESSON 7

DON'T JUDGE YOURSELF—OR PUT YOURSELF ON A PEDESTAL

One person's story is not more important or amazing than someone else's story.

Writing is not about being able to say: My secrets and traumas are bigger and more important than yours. Pain is pain is pain! Several years ago, I was at a retreat with more than a hundred people. I was asked to share what had been the secret of my life, giving a baby up for adoption, in front of everyone. It took everything for me to tell my story, and I broke down into tears as I finished. I was embraced by others and comforted and felt completely met. And then....someone else stood up and told her story, and she was embraced by others and comforted and met. It was in that moment I realized I had held my secret in such a way that I carried it with me everywhere! I actually thought my pain was greater than another's pain! Pain is pain, and there is enough love for all of us to be embraced.

Lesson 7 Exercises

- In what ways have you thought or felt that your pain or experiences were worse than anyone else's?

- Better?

- How are your experiences different or similar to the experiences of other people you know?

LESSON 8
STAY GROUNDED IN THE PRESENT

Writing your story isn't about feeling bad all over again about unhappy experiences. It's about exploring what part of you may have disappeared when it could no longer tell the truth.

I was seeing an acupuncturist for the first time, and she was taking my history. She got to the part: How many children do you have? It was like time stood still, because I heard myself say: I have THREE children! I had always answered two. I burst into tears. It was the first time I had answered that question truthfully.

Lesson 8 Exercises

- What truths might you reveal as you write your story?

- How might this set you free?

- Describe any new emotions you are experiencing as you go through these exercises.

LESSON 9

BE PERSISTENT AND COURAGEOUS

Writing about your secrets and the lies you probably needed to tell to keep them is a lot of work. But if you can find the courage to reveal to yourself the truth you are holding just below the surface, I believe you'll begin to live a more fulfilled life, a life of freedom.

I had no idea that the eighteen-year-old me, who had given her baby up for adoption, was frozen in time emotionally. I didn't realize that the day I kept the secret of my daughter's birth was the day my emotional system stood still. After all, my energy was going into living as though it had never happened. Maybe it's time for you to "let go" and allow yourself to grow beyond the secrets you may be keeping.

Lesson 9 Exercises

- Is there a topic that you don't want to write about?

- Why?

- How can you dig deeper to free this story and the locked emotions that surround it?

_____

_____

_____

INVITE FORGIVENESS

Use your writing to invite forgiveness. Can you share your story?

The thought of sharing my story could bring me to my knees and make me feel like heaving! I have so much compassion for my younger self today. Why was I so hard on myself? Where did all that judgment come from? Have you been judging yourself harshly? Maybe it's time to write about your inner longings to be free and to forgive whatever needs to be forgiven and move on. When my supervisor in the chaplaincy program asked if I had forgiven myself, I had absolutely no idea how to do that. Writing and sharing your story is the beginning of forgiveness. When we read our words back to ourselves, we realize we are just human beings with strengths and weaknesses. No one is perfect. But our truthful stories ARE perfect!

Lesson 10 Exercises

- Is there something you haven't forgiven yourself for, or feel shame regarding?

- Or are you holding resentment towards someone else?

- Write about this, and open yourself to forgiveness as you write. Realize that you are not alone in having memories that may trap you in shame or anger, but that you can release them.

LESSON 11
KEEP MOVING FORWARD

Realize you have a message that someone needs to hear—and that someone may be you. Are you asking: What difference would it make to tell your story? You can't change anything that's happened in the past! Aren't you supposed to pick yourself up and go on?

That's exactly how I lived my life for many, many years. In one sentence I could use the words abandoned, shame, guilt, sorrow, remorse, despair, self-loathing, phony, fearful, and grief stricken to describe myself. WOW! That's what was living under the rock named "secrets and lies" that I was dragging behind me everywhere I went! As I mentioned earlier, writing and sharing my story was the beginning of forgiving myself. It allowed new words to describe me: released, freed, hopeful, happy, filled with joy, feeling authentic, and knowing my power. Isn't telling your story worth a try? Maybe you will find new and wonderful ways to describe yourself!

Lesson 11 Exercises

- How has your story kept you stuck with negative definitions of yourself?

- What new, positive definitions can you adopt?

- How might your story of redemption influence others who read it?

FIT YOUR STORY INTO YOUR LIFE

Realize that telling your story won't change everything, but it will start to change you. If I write my story, do I get to live happily ever after?

When I shared about giving my daughter up for adoption, I thought that was the biggest story I could ever tell. However, it was just the beginning of the story. Once I told the secret and forgave myself for the lies I told to keep that secret, I was inspired to look for and to be united with my daughter. Once the wheels were set in motion, we found each other rather easily. It was wonderful to meet her and the grandson I didn't know I had. But our relationship could never quite get off the ground—for many reasons that I share in this book. However, I can honestly tell you it was worth it—the whole shebang! Because I went into my story and dared to live through it and feel the truth that surfaced, my life is much happier today. No matter how the story ends, if it's your true story, then just maybe "happily ever after" is possible. For me, "happily ever after" is the freedom I feel being me.

Lesson 12 Exercises

- How is writing changing you?

- What does "happily ever after" look like to you, in relation to your story?

- How will you know when you can enter the last tipi for the last time because your story will be done?

This *Last Tipi* guide helps you engage your loved ones by bringing them into the last tipi to share the stories that shape their lives. As a former hospice chaplain, I listened to many end-of-life stories and realized, on a deeper level, the importance of telling one's story. The people I served taught me many things, but the most important thing I learned was that *each person has a story to tell and deserves to have that life witnessed.*

My hope is to inspire you to take that step—the step that might feel uncomfortable when engaging elders, people who are ill, and most importantly, people who have a short time to live—and realize that people tell stories in all kinds of ways. We need to leave our agendas at the door and be open to whatever they wish to share.

My early days as a chaplain were filled with self-doubt. I wondered if I ever was of any help to the people I met. During my training, I learned that I didn't know the effects of my own story, so I brought all my nerves and unresolved issues with me as I entered a patient's room. However, as time went on, I gained experience and confidence in my work and discovered that all I really needed to do was have peace and quiet within myself. I needed to offer space so that others could trust that I would listen.

That's all you need to do, too. Just offer yourself and provide space for your loved ones to share their stories. I hope *The Last Tipi* helps guide you on your journey.

LESSON 1
MEETING OUR FEAR

When I first began my training as a hospice chaplain, I was afraid to walk into a dying patient's room and begin a conversation. You may feel nervous, too, because it takes courage to begin conversations with people who are ill or coming to the end of life.

Writing about fear reminds me of when I was a teenager. I didn't know how to swim. At my first swimming lesson, the teacher brought me to the end of a pier and said, "Jump in!"

"But I don't know how to swim!" I exclaimed.

"I know," the teacher said, "but it's not until you jump in and get wet that you can begin to learn."

Lesson 1 Exercise

- Are you ready to "jump in" and find courage to speak to a loved one and invite him/her to share his/her story?

- What fears or insecurities do you have about this process? What holds you back?

- What do you hope to gain in this process—or how do you hope it will help your loved one? Reflect and record your answers.

LESSON 2
ALL KINDS OF WAYS TO
TELL A STORY—GLADYS'S STORY

I was assigned to a major medical center's long-term care/hospice floor early in my chaplaincy training. One day a week, I offered a prayer service for all who could attend. I was a little nervous, because I was new at such things. But as I watched people come into the activity room and gather around the big round table before me, my nerves fell away. These sweet people humbled me. They arrived with health aides and walkers—and some, like Gladys, entered in a wheelchair. I opened with a prayer of gratitude, and we each shared at least one thing we were grateful for. But Gladys didn't speak. I read a story from *Chicken Soup for the Soul,* and everyone loved the happy ending of the fireman rescuing a kitten in a tree.

As we were discussing the story, some people in the room said they hoped someone would come and save them too, because they felt trapped just like that kitten. Still, Gladys didn't speak. In fact, Gladys looked sound asleep. She was tethered to her chair, and it seemed to be the only thing keeping her from falling to the floor.

I closed our prayer meeting with the song "Amazing Grace." This choice was met with smiles and affirmations, and we all began to sing. Suddenly, to everyone's surprise, we heard a soft, sweet voice singing along with us. It was Gladys! She knew every word of the song! We were truly amazed that day. Everyone began to clap for Gladys, and she looked at us and smiled. A sweet soul at the table reached over to touch Gladys's arm and said: "That song must really mean something to you!" Gladys simply smiled and nodded her head.

When we have loved ones dealing with dementia and Alzheimer's disease, it often seems impossible for them to share their stories. I think Gladys's story is an example of the importance of including these dear folks in our family circles. While they may not be able to write their stories with thousands of words, there are still meaningful ways for them to express themselves—while providing glimpses into who they are and the lives they've lived. It may come through playing or singing a song, engaging in an art project, or showing photographs. I learned that we never know what remembrance is just beneath the surface, waiting for the right song to be sung!

Lesson 2 Exercise

- How can YOU engage your loved one dealing with dementia or Alzheimer's disease—or another limitation?

- What music or visual cue might help trigger productive emotions for your loved one?

- How can you capture the spirit of your loved one's response, even if you can't write down words? (Consider using a recording device, photographs, or video to capture your loved one's responses as you help him or her explore memories.)

THE GIFT OF OUR STORIES —DONALD'S STORY

For more than a year, I visited Donald. He was completely bedridden and could no longer speak…but his eyes were always alert! I would go into his room and say: "Hello, Donald. It's good to see you today!" And Donald would close his eyes. Week after week, month after month, Donald closed his eyes…until one day, he kept them open. I almost didn't know what to say, because we had never gotten that far before. Donald turned his eyes to the side of the room where there was a table, and I followed with my eyes. On the table was a box. I asked if he wanted me to get the box. He blinked his eyes, and I assumed it meant yes.

I got the box and asked if he wanted me to open it. He blinked again. The box was filled with newspaper articles and pictures of his family, including his grandchildren. He also had a picture of a fine home on a hill. The newspaper article spoke about Donald being a town selectman, and he even had owned his own business. I could hardly believe all that was inside the box…a whole life story of a beautiful man who had lived a wonderful life before I had met him.

I learned from Donald that within all of us is a "box" that holds the gift of our stories, and I thought of the people who had lovingly taken the time to create the treasures of his story so he could share them with me.

Lesson 3 Exercise

- How can YOU help a family member or friend gather their precious mementos?

- What items might go into a treasure box? What feelings or memories might these evoke?

- How can you alert caregivers and other loved ones to get to know your loved one through this treasure box?

_____

_____

_____

_____

_____

_____

_____

_____

_____

_____

_____

_____

LESSON 4
RECLAIMING POWER, ANN'S STORY

In Chapter 8, I mention Ann, a woman in her late thirties with brain cancer. Each time I would visit her, she would greet me with a big smile and tell me she was doing JUST GREAT! She answered me this way for some time, until one day when I entered her room I found her crying. Family and friends had just been to see her, but she seemed sad instead of happy after their visit.

"Ann," I asked, "what seems to be the matter?"

"Sometimes it just seems so hard to keep smiling when I'm really crying inside," she told me.

When I first offered that she might want to share her real feelings with her family and friends the next time they came to see her, with tears streaming down her beautiful face, she told me, "Oh no, Kris, I couldn't do that, because then they would feel sad, too."

In the days that followed, I met with Ann's family and friends and asked them how their visits with Ann were going. They were able to tell me that it had become really hard to stay "upbeat" because they'd been visiting her for so long and knew she would not be coming home to them. Ann had been living on the hospice unit for more than six months. They felt it was their obligation to be cheerful, otherwise Ann would feel sad.

It seemed to me that no one was able to say how he or she was truly feeling. So during my next visit with Ann, I asked her if she would like to share her story and write to the people she loved in a way that would express how she felt about them. In this way, she could leave them something from her heart, while telling them how much they meant to her. To my surprise, her face lit up!

"I'd love to do this, Kris, but I can't write anymore," she told me. The solution was simple: I offered to write down the messages she wanted to share.

Ann became excited about this very real act of living. For weeks, during our visits, Ann would give me names of friends and family she wanted to write to. She would dictate her thoughts and make revisions along the way. She would tell me, "Oh, that's what I've always wanted to tell (her or him)."

And she would thank me for the chance to share her feelings.

The day came when her "story" was complete, and I told her I would type it up and give it to her family when the time came of her passing. With great authority, she told me, "Oh no, Kris, I don't want my family and friends to wait to know how I feel about them; I want to read this to them now!"

Wow! This really surprised me, because Ann had been so afraid to say how she felt just a few short weeks before. Yet now, she was saying that she actually wanted to read her feelings out loud. And…she wanted me to invite all of the people on her list to the hospital so she could read her thoughts with everyone she cared about surrounding her. I told her I'd see what I could do.

I brought this news to the nursing staff, and it was met with amazement and real joy. They told me they felt that Ann had been using all of her strength to bolster everyone's feelings, and as a result, her own feelings had been neglected. One nurse shared with me, "This writing project has allowed Ann to be who she really is: a courageous woman on an amazing journey. By telling her story, her spirit seems to have been lifted, and she has lifted ours too."

We made arrangements for Ann's family and friends to meet in an unoccupied laundry room. When I told them what Ann wanted to do, many of them seemed scared.

"What does she want to say to me?"

"What am I supposed to do?"

"What will I say to her?"

"I feel like crying already!"

The nurses were scared, too. For days, they would whisper to me,

"Can Ann really handle this?"

"Is this too much for her family?"

"What are WE supposed to do?"

Their nerves were spilling out everywhere. Even I was a little nervous. None of us had been part of a gathering like this before. The one who kept smiling with anticipation, however, was Ann.

"Oh Kris, I can hardly wait for everyone to come. Do you think we could have a few treats for people after I speak?"

The day finally arrived. People were streaming down the corridor…each one looking more afraid than the last. We entered the tiny laundry room where all the supplies had been pushed against the walls. I wheeled Ann into the center of the room, and we encircled her.

With the brightest smile you can imagine, she sat there with her written story in her hands and began speaking to the first person on her list. She didn't get very far before we all burst into tears, including the staff.

Ann was magnificent as she went from person to person, sharing her love for each and expressing gratitude for all the time and effort they had given her while she was in the hospital. Ann made it clear how important they each were in her life.

Ann's story of love and courage made a difference to every person who was in the room that day, including me.

Several months after Ann shared her story in that tiny laundry room with all of us surrounding her, she died. At the ceremony of the celebration of her life, I was greeted by Ann's family and friends.

With tears streaming down their smiling faces, they shared that Ann's act of telling her story before she died was deeply meaningful and that the memory of her joy at being able to tell them how she felt had moved them deeply. It was an experience they would never forget.

I learned there are many ways to "experience" a person's story. The stories I've shared with you in Guide #2 offer examples of the many layers of communicating and listening.

GLADYS simply needed to hear the right sound to find the song within her that told us she had a song to sing. She was WITNESSED that day.

DONALD was finally able to trust enough to allow the box holding the stories of his life to be opened. He was SEEN.

ANN needed to express her honest feelings and share them with her family and friends. She was finally HEARD.

Lesson 4 Exercise

- Who do YOU know who is waiting to be witnessed, seen, and heard?

- What is the best method to help your loved one tell a story or feel recognized and heard?

- How can you act on this to make it a reality in the coming weeks?

_____

_____

_____

_____

_____

_____

_____

_____

_____

_____

_____

_____

_____

LESSON 5

THE IMPORTANCE OF TELLING OUR STORIES

Today, there is growing recognition of the importance of storytelling, and it's changing the way doctors treat illness!

Realizing that simply taking down data about a patient's medical history did not tell the whole story about that patient's health, a program called Narrative Medicine has been developed by Dr. Rita Charon at Columbia University in New York. New doctors take courses in literature to better familiarize themselves with the art of telling a story to help them connect with a world—a patient's world—other than their own.

Similar programs exist across the country. In fact, the Memorial Sloan-Kittering Cancer Center in New York has a program called Visible Ink wherein patients are paired with writing coaches to work on projects that help with self-expression and stress reduction.

The medical field is beginning to understand that telling and listening to stories is the way we make sense of our lives.

Lesson 5 Exercise

- Can YOU lift out of your own story and make the leap into "another world" to help your loved one tell his/her story? What shift needs to occur in you to make this happen?

- What reading or learning opportunities might help you prepare for this role?

_____

_____

_____

_____

_____

_____

_____

_____

_____

_____

_____

_____

_____

_____

_____

_____

LESSON 6
THE HEALING POWER OF WRITING

Dr. Lewis Mehl-Madrona is certified in psychiatry, family practice, and geriatrics, and worked for years in rural emergency medicine. In his book: *Healing the Mind Through the Power of Story*, he writes, "Written language has been shown to have great healing power. People who write about deep personal topics have highly significant changes in clinically relevant measures." In other words, the quality of life and the potential for healing rises when patients are able to WRITE their stories.

Lesson 6 Exercise

- How might helping your loved one WRITE his/her story improve his/her health or well-being?

_____

_____

_____

_____

_____

_____

_____

LESSON 7
SEASONS OF SURVIVORSHIP

Dr. Phil Glynn, Director of Oncology at Mercy Medical Center in Springfield, Massachusetts, held a seminar I attended titled, "Seasons of Survivorship—A Patient's Journey Through Diagnosis, Treatment and Beyond." Dr. Glynn believes there is an incredible need for support from people who have gone through the experience of dealing with a life-threatening experience.

The first two speakers were doctors who had survived cancer. They told of all the support they received during their diagnosis, surgery, and physical therapy, and how once that was done, they were on their own. They felt abandoned and lonely with doctors and family expecting them to "get back to normal." What was normal anymore? One way to deal with their emotional journey was to write their stories and share them with family members.

I was the third speaker. As a former hospice chaplain, I offered that suffering changes us. I quoted Paul Tillich, a Jesuit theologian, who wrote about suffering. He said that when someone has deeply suffered, that person finds a self within that they never knew existed. It is THAT self that has a story to tell.

Today, Mercy Medical Center has introduced projects that encourage their cancer patients to write and share their stories.

Lesson 7 Exercise

- Do YOU have a loved one who has journeyed through diagnosis, treatment, and beyond? How will you help this person tell the story?

- How might your support help this person process an untold story?

LESSON 8
DYING WITHOUT REGRET

The word "REGRET" comes from the Middle English word "regretten," meaning "to weep."

Regret is natural and part of the human condition.

The question is: will we keep our regrets or let them go? People facing the end of life often have memories arise about unresolved issues and events.

"If only I hadn't…"

"If only I had…"

"I'd give anything if…"

Helping our loved ones release regrets helps break the chains of the past. If your loved one is open to sharing his/ her regrets, simply help them to:

Describe

Examine

Grieve

Let It Go

Lesson 8 Exercise

- How can YOU help a loved one release regrets by telling his/ her story?

- How might this person be transformed by releasing those regrets?

- What questions can you ask to help this person tell such stories?

LESSON 9

THE TOP FIVE REGRETS OF THE DYING

Australian nurse Bronnie Ware spent several years working in palliative care, caring for patients in the last twelve weeks of their lives. She wrote about her experiences in a blog that became so popular that she ultimately wrote a book called *The Top Five Regrets of the Dying*. Some of the regrets she shared in the book are:

1. I wish I'd had the courage to live a life true to myself...not the life others expected of me.

2. I wish I hadn't worked so hard.

3. I wish I'd had the courage to express my feelings.

4. I wish I had stayed in touch with my friends.

5. I wish I had let myself be happier.

Lesson 9 Exercise

- Do YOU have a loved one nearing the end of life? Are you willing to listen to this person's regrets?

- Are you able to allow his/her feelings and not try to make things "better"?

- What fears or personal limitations might you need to overcome in order to best facilitate the story mining process?

LESSON 10
THREE SIMPLE
THINGS TO REMEMBER

Three simple things to remember when helping loved ones share stories:

1. It doesn't matter what story they tell!

2. Offer to write or record their stories!

3. Invite them to share their stories with family and friends.

Lesson 10 Exercise

•   How can YOU begin the process of helping your loved one share his/her story?

•   What is the best method to get started? Can you pre-write questions to get the ball rolling, starting with easy questions that are less emotional…and leading up to questions that may reveal regrets? (If your loved one is having trouble getting started, I suggest asking him/her to describe childhood and adolescence, including the key characters—like family members. Next, ask your loved one to describe feelings associated with that time of life—favorite activities, things the family enjoyed, and anything that was hard on the family.)

LESSON 11
BE A COMPASSIONATE LISTENER

Sometimes we think only people who are chaplains, priests, rabbis, or trained counselors are qualified to listen to people's stories. But that's not true! Every one of us has the capacity to sit with someone who needs to talk, tell a story, or simply be comforted. Listening IS compassionate!

As with Gladys, Donald, and Ann, listening to your loved ones helps them to feel:

WITNESSED

SEEN

HEARD

Lesson 11 Exercise

• Is there a Gladys, a Donald, or an Ann in your life —a family member, friend, or acquaintance? Are YOU a compassionate listener? How can you improve your listening skills to draw out this person's story?

_____

_____

_____

_____

LESSON 12
WHAT TO REMEMBER

1. Remember that everyone has a story to tell.

2. Regrets are about being human.

3. Releasing secrets and regrets allows for healing.

The more in touch YOU are with YOUR secrets and regrets, the more able you are to:

WITNESS

SEE

HEAR

the stories of your loved ones.

Lesson 12 Exercise

- Are YOU ready to begin helping a loved one tell his/her story? Are there any stories that you need to tell first to "clear the palate" so that you can listen to someone else's victories, regrets, and wishes?

_____

_____

_____

_____

_____

WHY HELPING YOUR LOVED ONE TELL A STORY IS IMPORTANT

Gladys, Donald, and Ann are a few of the many faces of storytelling. When I was a hospice chaplain, they taught me to leave my story at the door and be open to whatever they wanted to share with me. Sometimes patients I visited didn't want to talk at all—and that was fine! As with Donald, I visited him for more than a year before he invited me to share in the story of his life. My point here is to meet people where they are.

I mentioned Dr. Mehl-Madrona in Lesson #6. Although he would prescribe medication when necessary, he had a rule patients had to follow if they wanted him to be their physician. They had to agree to meet once a week with him and other patients, and tell their stories. Having worked with many indigenous people, he knows how powerful the story of "our tribe"—our family—is and that storytelling brings meaning to people's lives.

As a nation, we are aging, and there are millions of people with stories to tell and wisdom to share. There are those who have held secrets and regrets for most of their lives, never living in a freer way. There are those who are aged. Family and friends have slipped away, and there is no one to listen to them. There are those who know their lives are ending and feel the need to share that ONE story that was never told.

Your role as a compassionate listener is very important. You have the power to help your loved ones, the elderly, and those facing death to feel that their lives have meaning.

Lesson 13 Exercise

- WHAT CAN YOU DO………..
- HOW CAN YOU DO IT……

_____

_____

_____

_____

_____

_____

_____

_____

_____

_____

_____

_____

I wrote a guide to help you tell your story first. Then I wrote a guide to help you guide friends and loved ones to tell their stories. And just when I thought I had exhausted this line of thinking, I got a message from my editor telling me that her 18-year-old step-daughter had been found dead from an overdose. She told me that her husband wanted to go into *the last tipi* and tell his daughter's story. This touched my heart so deeply that I decided to create a guide to help people tell the story of a loved one who has passed.

I called my friend, Jan, and asked if she would help me create a guide to help people tell the story of a loved one who had passed by first telling the story of her 9-year-old granddaughter, who had died from brain cancer three years before. She agreed, and I'm grateful to her for her courage and willingness to share her journey.

I hope the journey Jan took with me helps you begin the process, when you are ready, of telling the story of a loved one you have lost. I believe it's in the telling of the story that the memory of our loved ones stays alive.

Nothing in life prepares us for losing someone we love.

What we are left with, the stories, is what helps heal wounds of loss. It keeps them alive and gives us strength to go on. Follow Jan's story, and envision yourself telling the story of your loved one who has passed.

LESSON 1
HOW DO I BEGIN?

I was new to the family when we found out that my husband's daughter was pregnant. Not having children of my own, I was thrilled I would get to be a part of a new baby's life! The first thing we did was buy a wonderful teddy bear for this soon to be born baby. I never expected to feel so much love for another human being before she was born! My heart just exploded, and I couldn't wait to meet this little girl.

Lesson 1 Exercise

- Tell the story of who *you* are and how the person you lost fit into your life.

- What did this person mean to you?

- How did this person change your life?

_____

_____

_____

_____

_____

WHO IS THE PERSON
WHO HAS PASSED?

They named the baby Caitlin! We met her when she was eight days old, and it was love at first sight. From the beginning, she was so pretty and alert, and she let everyone hold her, including me! I got to visit her on holidays and at family gatherings. I started a doll collection for her, adding to it on each birthday. I loved her, because she was part of my husband and, by default, part of me. I couldn't stop buying her clothes! Caitlin was a complete joy—beautiful, incredibly smart, sweet, funny, and silly. She had a laugh that filled a room, and she loved to sing!

When Caitlin was five years old, she was having vision problems and had been to several doctors to figure out the cause. After she had an MRI, it was discovered she had a large brain tumor. The day she was operated on was the longest day of my life. She spent eleven weeks in the hospital and endured rounds of radiation and chemotherapy. The chemotherapy lasted for three years.

My world as I knew it stopped. I became part of a "round robin" of grandparents spending two weeks at a time with her, her little brother, and her family. Here was this little girl, so courageous and brave, and all of us trying not to show our fear of losing her. Through all of this, Caitlin was incredibly positive and incredibly sweet.

Lesson 2 Exercise

- Tell the story of who *your lost loved* one was. What did this person teach you?

- What did you most admire about this person?

_____

_____

_____

_____

_____

_____

_____

_____

_____

_____

_____

_____

_____

_____

WHAT WERE YOU FEELING WHEN YOU KNEW YOUR LOVED ONE WOULD PASS ON?

Almost five years after her initial diagnosis, Caitlin had a recurrence of brain cancer. We had been told that if it came back, there would be very little they could do for her. This was the sweet little girl who called me Nana; who loved books, purses, and birds; whose favorite color was purple; who wanted to be an astronaut...and she was leaving us. I still don't have words that truly describe the loss I was feeling. I kept thinking: She's too young to die! How will we live without her?

Lesson 3 Exercise

- How did it affect you to know for the first time that your loved one would pass on (or had passed on)? How did this change you?

- What did this bring up about your own mortality?

_____

_____

_____

_____

LESSON 4
HOW DO YOU THINK YOUR LOVED ONE CHANGED THE WORLD?

Caitlin never met a stranger. She smiled at everyone. She would sing in public with sweet abandon. She took my husband and me to lunch one day and insisted that she pay for lunch with her own credit card. With a "wink" to the waitress, Caitlin gave her "credit card" to pay the bill. She left that day feeling very grown up, believing she had paid for our lunch.

Her Make-A-Wish trip was to see a space shuttle launch. She wanted to be an astronaut! I have a picture of her family at the launch site. Everyone is looking at the camera, but Caitlin is looking the other way—at the space shuttle launching into space.

Once, when she was very young, Caitlin called us on the phone and said: "I have a story to tell you, and it's going to take seventeen minutes!" That's who she was—a happy little girl who had something to say and must have known she only had so much time to say it.

She made the world at large a better place, and she has made my world a better place, too.

Lesson 4 Exercise

- Did your loved one change you and your world? How?

LESSON 5
AFTER YOUR LOVED ONE PASSED, WERE YOU ABLE TO EXPRESS YOUR GRIEF?

It seemed that ALL I could feel was grief. Caitlin was not my biological granddaughter, but in my mind and heart, I lost my granddaughter. I was heartbroken. Nothing in my life had prepared me for losing this dear child. Caitlin's mother, father, and brother were suffering. My husband's family and all of Caitlin's grandparents were suffering. I was suffering, too.

I went through all the stages of grief they tell you about, and sometimes I went through them again. My anger that this child could die this way was real. How could I ever resign myself to this loss?

It's been a little more than three years since Caitlin died. I am finally able to talk about her without bursting into tears, but they are never far from the surface. It may always be this way.

Lesson 4 Exercise

* Are you able to express your grief?

* Where are you now with your grief?

* If you are having trouble expressing your grief, is there someone you can seek out to share it with? This may be a grief group, counselor, pastor, friend, or family member. You may want to try different avenues of expression until you find the one(s) that feel beneficial.

IF YOUR LOVED ONE WAS SITTING BESIDE YOU TODAY, WHAT WOULD YOU TELL HIM OR HER?

I would tell her she lit up my life! I would thank her for embracing me as Nana! I would tell her she was a gift I never expected to receive! I would bow to her courage! I would say thank you, thank you, thank you for opening my heart to the purest love there is! I would tell her how much I loved her over and over again.

Lesson 6 Exercise

- What would you tell your loved one?

- Would you talk about happy memories? Would you share pictures and tell stories? Write or speak what you would say as if your loved one could hear you now.

_____

_____

_____

_____

_____

LESSON 7
HOW CAN YOU KEEP YOUR LOVED ONE ALIVE WITHIN YOU?

I have so many cute, sweet stories to share about Caitlin. I have cards she wrote to me, the pictures we took over the years, and so many wonderful memories. When I talk about Caitlin, it's as though she's right here beside me. When I share about the love I have for her, I can feel it expanding my heart.

Lesson 7 Exercise

- Gather keepsakes that mattered to you and your loved one. What are they, and why are they significant? What memories do you have around these keepsakes? How can you honor them now?

- Write the stories that sing in your heart when you think of your loved one. Can you set aside a special book to write these thoughts and stories as they come to you? Create a book of remembrance that celebrates your loved ones life and the significance that person had in your life! You can add pictures, keepsakes, and words to keep it alive. Come back and visit it when you want to feel close to your loved one.

HOW DOES LIFE GO ON?

There is, of course, an empty space within me since Caitlin died. I try to fill it with happy memories and remember to be grateful for the gift of time we had with her. Some days are better than others. Gathering the keepsakes that mattered to me and to Caitlin helps make our relationship stay alive. The happy times did happen. I did love her. She did love me. I will always know this, and it's that love that sustains me.

Lesson 8 Exercise

- Now that you have recalled them, can you tell the stories of the loved one you have lost to others? Telling their stories keeps "them" alive and gives you strength to go on without them.

- Who can you tell a story to this week, to help keep the memories alive? Be open to hearing words of comfort from this person who listens to the story.

LESSON 9
DO THE PAIN AND GRIEF EVER END?

I don't think pain and grief ever end, but they begin to form shades of grey. Caitlin is out of pain, and that is a good thing. I simply miss her—her impromptu phone calls, her laughter and ability to make my day sweeter. I deal with my pain and grief by focusing on all the positive things she was and brought into our lives. Although her loss is unbearable most days, very often a streak of joy will cross my heart as I realize she came into this world to bring love, joy, and excitement about life to everyone she met. When I think about that, I know she did what she came here to do.

Lesson 9 Exercise

- Everyone is different processing grief. How is it for you?

- What has helped you most in processing your grief?

- In what new area do you feel called to express or process your grief? Be gentle with yourself. It takes time to process such an unimaginable loss.

WILL TELLING THE STORY OF A LOVED ONE'S PASSING SOOTHE AND HEAL THE HEART, OR WILL IT MAKE THE PAIN RETURN?

I think initially I thought it would make the pain return. My husband wondered if it was too much for me to handle. But I have enjoyed going over all the pictures we have of her and rereading the notes and cards she sent. Putting all of our keepsakes together and creating a "Caitlin storybook" has made me happy—happy to honor her life, happy to honor our relationship. It's something I can hold in my hands and hold close to my heart, and it is soothing to me.

The "Caitlin storybook" marks a beginning and an end to her time here with us, but it also reflects how my heart has been touched—and she will live in that heart forever!

Lesson 10 Exercise

- Holding in pain may harm you in unseen ways. Are you holding in your pain?

- Sharing the story allows you to be seen and heard. Do you have a friend or loved one to listen to your story?

- Sharing the story of a loved one's passing may bring sad feelings to the surface, but in sharing your feelings, the heart has a chance to heal. Do you have the courage to tell your loved one's story and allow yourself to begin the healing process?

A FINAL WORD

Chapter 1 of my story begins with: What Does A Chaplain Do? I've ended this book with ways to be the chaplain—your own chaplain—a compassionate listener — and have a little help on what to do, how to tell your own story and the story of others you care about.

Like the many in this book—including myself—I invite you to spend time in the last tipi and gently encourage your stories to come forward. We see the world through the stories we tell ourselves, and if those stories no longer serve us, we could be missing the good things that come our way. Tell your old story for the last time, leave it in the last tipi, and get ready to be free to write a new one.

Or help someone else tell an important story, even if it is too late for the subject of the story. All of us fear heartbreak. The loss of a loved one strips away everything that is no longer important, and leaves us raw in the essence of who we truly are. We are left with stories that keep our loved ones alive in that broken open place, and that is what helps us to heal and go on with our lives. Jan's story of her granddaughter, Caitlin, illustrates the courage it takes to face our own broken hearts, because working our way through tragic losses is an inevitable part of our human journey.

May you find blessings along the way.

ABOUT THE AUTHOR

Kris Landry is an author, speaker, healer, and coach whose life journey is marked by her diverse roles—from professional singer, to chaplain, to her current mission of guiding others to healing through telling their stories.

Kris started her career in music—singing on stage at eleven years old; attending the Boston Conservatory of Music as a teenager; singing professionally with a folk group; and appearing on television, radio, and news print across the US. She was a church soloist for thirty years— known as "the wedding singer"—and released two CDs as a fundraiser to help build a vocational school in India for displaced Tibetans.

Having graduated from Mount Holyoke College and earning a master's degree from Boston College, she also trained to become a Certified Catholic Chaplain—working with hospice patients in their final days. While there, she developed a deep heart for helping people tell their final stories—and grew the courage to tell her own personal story of releasing her daughter for adoption.

In recent years, Kris has worked with energy healers in America and Europe; studied healing and energy techniques in Santa Fe, NM, with a renowned teacher; and currently has a healing practice for people who have experienced trauma, stress, surgery, and the effects of chemotherapy. She has also completed certification and training in Tibetan Soul Healing: *Tse Dup Jha Ri Ma.*

Kris lives her mission of helping people through humanitarian pursuits, including sponsoring a young woman who resides at Menri Monastery in India, and building of an extension to the nunnery at Menri Monastery in India to provide school space for the young nuns and living space for her sponsored daughter, Yangchen.

Kris has been married for fifty years and has three children.

To connect or learn more about Kris, visit www.TheLastTipi.com.

ACKNOWLEDGMENTS

The arc of writing *THE LAST TIPI* covers fifteen years of stops, starts, editing, revisions, and emerging personal stories that begged to be included. I want to thank everyone who had a part in supporting this effort. I could write stories about each and every person whose expertise and support helped me through the completion of this book, but that might take another fifteen years. So with deep affection and gratitude, I'd simply like to thank Victoria Wright, George Foster, Wendy-Lipton Dibner, Tim Boden, and Jocelyn Godfrey.

Special thanks to Ilizabeth Fortune, who dared me to complete this work and bring it to the world.

Thanks to my amazing family and friends, who read and reread the many editions of *The Last Tipi* and encouraged me to tell *the whole story.*

Thank you to my husband, Larry, without whom I could never have taken this journey.

And, of course, thank you to all my children.

41609310R00167

Made in the USA
Middletown, DE
18 March 2017